B3

The Gerald Ford Letters

THE
GERALD FORD
LETTERS

Robert N. Winter-Berger

Lyle Stuart, Inc. ∘ Secaucus, New Jersey

Library of Congress Catalog No. 74-81720
Copyright © 1974 by Robert N. Winter-Berger
All Rights Reserved
Printed in the United States of America

ISBN No. 0-8184-0204-0

To Esther and Tony and all my other friends who remained loyal to me during my difficult quest to tell the truth.

"I scarcely know Robert N. Winter-Berger. I may have met him eight or ten times. I may have written to him five or six times."

Gerald Rudolph Ford

"I sometimes saw Jerry Ford as often as seven or eight times a month—over a three and a half year period. A lobbyist's job is most often done verbally with the legislator who is doing him a favor. As little as possible is put in writing, for the obvious reason. Even so, Jerry Ford wrote to me and my clients some fifty times."

Robert N. Winter-Berger

The Gerald Ford Letters

Publisher's Foreword

In January of 1972, following a series of events that will be described in the pages that follow, I became the publisher of a book titled *The Washington Pay-Off* by Robert N. Winter-Berger.

My publishing companies have been built largely on controversy. We rush in where angels fear to tread. In an industry dominated by giants, our medium-sized publishing complex is able to compete because we offer a combination of ingredients that aren't elsewhere: courage and integrity.

We made a success of *The Washington Pay-Off* despite the press blackout that you will read about in these pages.

I am not much concerned with book reviewers. Like the little boy who knew that the emperor was naked, I know them for what they are: pretenders, eunuchs, and fakes. The exceptions exist but they are rare.

It was no surprise, for example, when reviewers ignored a book as important as *The Rich and the*

Super-Rich by Ferdinand Lundberg. This one received only two major reviews. One was a hatchet job by a man who was one of those criticized in the pages of the book. The other concentrated on a single error (a wealthy man had died a year before but was described in the book as presiding over his holdings) in a 950-page volume with 4,000-plus facts, and ballooned that error into a total ridicule of the book.

Despite this, *The Rich and the Super-Rich* became the number one best seller in America for many months.

It's been that way with book after book. *The Sensuous Woman* has sold something like ten million copies in the United States alone. It changed the sex habits of millions of women. Its impact on films, books, magazines, newspapers, and even on television has been tremendous. Yet it was never reviewed by the *New York Times*. It might have been if the imprint had been Harper's or Knopf or Random House. They're the fellows who throw the elaborate cocktail parties, take the reviewers to lunch at the Italian Pavilion, and otherwise pamper them and pander to their pomposity—and they apparently do it without conscience or qualm.

All of this by way of explaining that when *The Washington Pay-Off* was scheduled to appear, we knew we could not depend on reviews. We had to make the book known through advertising. We did.

At that time, Americans were apathetic. A poll

showed that fewer than three percent of all adult voters considered "corruption" an important issue.

Lincoln Steffens, Ida Tarbell, and Upton Sinclair would have had to become shoe clerks to survive if they'd written their muckraking classics today.

Nevertheless, *The Washington Pay-Off* had a decided impact. Making it known was a struggle, but we won.

It was also pre-Watergate. It was before the world learned that Spiro Agnew was a grafter and Richard Nixon a liar and a thief. So it was that many tell me now that they read the book with a jaundiced eye and a (not unhealthy) measure of disbelief.

In the final issue of his newsletter, *in Fact*, George Seldes, a journalistic crusader and hero, quoted Romain Rolland as saying, "Never tire of protesting." Seldes titled his own autobiography *Tell the Truth and Run.*

Winter-Berger told the truth, and there was dead silence in the auditorium. Nobody wanted to hear the truth. He protested but people had other important things on their minds — like football games and the Johnny Carson show.

I won't spill the story. At many points it becomes a cliff-hanger. But I do want to say that before we followed through on the creation of the book you hold in your hands, I made dead certain that what it contains is Truth.

Being human, Winter-Berger is fallible. He is as imperfect as any of us. There were some contradictions, omissions, self-serving memory lapses in what he said about some of his former political friends in *The Washington Pay-Off*. His feelings in the beginning were understandably ambivalent. Should he tell the whole unvarnished truth? Or, should he soften the blow, as he did in some cases?

I don't think you'll find any of that hesitancy in these pages.

Just as Bob Winter-Berger was about to begin this book, I told it to him straight. The dialogue went as follows, and I'll report it without laundering it.

Stuart: "Bob, I don't care what you've done in the past. I do care about what you're about to do. I want you to know that if you lie anywhere in this book—if you willfully deceive me or the reader in any way— I'm going to punch your fucking head off."

Winter-Berger: "I understand."

When this script was finished, I told Winter-Berger that he would have to take one of those lie

14

detector tests that he had unsuccessfully challenged Gerald Ford to take.

He took not one, but two.

I wanted to be convinced.

Among the questions asked during both tests were "Did you give Gerald Ford cash?" and "Did Gerald Ford take the money?"

The polygraphs showed a perfect score for "telling the truth" on both answers. And the answers were "Yes."

The man who conducted the first test is one of the foremost authorities in the field. His reputation is international. I was therefore particularly curious to know his personal feelings apart from the positive polygraph results.

His comment, "Entirely credible."

Your witness.

Lyle Stuart

Port Maria
Jamaica, W.I.
April 25, 1974

Book One

CHAPTER ONE

I became a lobbyist in 1964 because it seemed to me to be a natural extension of the public relations work that I was doing in New York. I quit lobbying in 1969.

During those five years, I saw and participated in a great number of things that fascinated me and some that appalled me. I was part of the process. I curried favor with congressmen. I did favors. I passed gifts. I conned clients, and I conned senators and representatives. In other words, I was a player in the game, and I played by its rules.

Perhaps if I had been a highly successful lobbyist, I might never have written a book. But I achieved only modest success. I am "meant to swell a crowd or two" rather than to stand at the head of an army, sword in hand, and lead the way.

Like most human beings, I am both very simple and very complex. If you asked me my motivations in writing *The Washington Pay-Off*, I would like to be able to say in all truth, "I did it only for my country. I did it only for the public good."

But I would not be leveling with you. I did do it for

17

those reasons. I also did it because I thought it would earn me some income—and because I needed income. I am not a wealthy man. Nor do I have that talent that many men have for scooping up riches as they saunter through life.

My motivations became secondary to the meaning and effect of what I wrote.

If a Mafia don decided to spill it all because he thought certain Mafia activities should be curbed, people would take seriously what he said. They would be concerned with his revelations. Only those whose lives were threatened by the exposé would say, "Don't pay any attention to him. He's Mafia. He's dirty."

I was in a dirty business. Lobbying—the kind that I was involved with—is one of the dirtiest. Its methods are entirely counter to the essence of democracy. It says, in effect, "All men are not equal. The courtrooms, judges, legislators—all government machines—are designed to grant special favors to the specially favored and to do the bidding of those who put the pennies in the slots. If this favored treatment goes against the public interest or makes one group an aristocracy of privilege and another mere peasants, then screw the public."

Corruption is not new. It is as old as recorded history. It exists everywhere. What is new, and sad, is the widespread acceptance of corruption as the American way of government.

18

So it was that I wrote my book. I knew I wouldn't come out of its pages looking like "Mr. Clean." But I hoped that what I looked like wouldn't be the paramount issue. I would tell a great deal of what I knew and hope that the information would be used effectively and constructively.

II

Toni Strassman is a literary agent whom I've known for twenty years. At the time I decided to tell what I knew, Toni was one of the few people with whom I was acquainted in the publishing business.

I spoke with Toni. She asked me to write a page or two explaining what I wanted to do and outlining the proposed book project.

I prepared the outline and gave it to her. She said it wasn't professionally done and that I should seek assistance. She suggested Glenn Kittler.

Toni arranged for an early evening meeting with Kittler at the office of his literary agent, also a woman. There, the four of us discussed the project.

Kittler was an editor of *Coronet* and had written more than a dozen books under his own name and claimed to have ghostwritten a number of others.

He made a good first impression, largely because we seemed to have the same sense of humor. Also, the subject matter appeared to excite him.

At our next meeting, we signed an agreement whereby Kittler would assist me in writing a book and would share equally in the proceeds.

Together we prepared a new outline and one chapter.

In July 1970, I recalled having met book publisher Bernard Geis several months before at the home of Richard and Pauline Ney. Toni didn't consider him a "proper" publisher, so without her approval, I called him, made an appointment, visited his office, and left the chapter and outline.

A week or two later, I phoned Geis. He said that he was interested. We set an appointment so that Kittler, myself, our two agents, and Geis could meet.

At that meeting, we argued out the terms of an agreement for the publication of a book. A week later, in August of 1970, we received actual contracts. The checks came. Twenty-five hundred dollars was divided in half and then agent commissions were deducted so that my share was $1,125. The Geis agreement called for total advances against royalties of $10,000, and I took a pencil and figured out this would mean a total of $4,500 for me, just a little above the annual poverty wage. Since I anticipated that it would take nine months to a year to prepare a finished manuscript, the initial rewards didn't seem unduly high.

We were eager to get going. The arrangement was that I would write during the week. We'd meet Thursdays, and Kittler and I would review what I'd written. Then he'd take it with him and work it over.

In six weeks, we completed four chapters. These were turned in to Geis.

Another payment of $2,500 was due.

We sweated out the next four weeks. Geis explained the delay by saying that his attorney, Maxwell Raab of the firm of Stroock, Stroock, and Lavan was out of town.

At a social gathering a couple of weeks later, I ran into one of Raab's partners. "I understand that Maxwell Raab is out of town. I wish he'd get back. I'm waiting for him, because Bernie Geis, who's your client, says he needs Raab's okay."

"Damn it, I wish Geis would stop telling people he's our client. Bernie Geis isn't a client of ours. And Max isn't out of town."

He was obviously annoyed that Geis had used the company name.

I telephoned Geis the next day. "I understand that Raab is back in town. Now can we get a quick decision?"

Geis said he'd get back to me in a day or two.

He did. He told me he'd decided against publishing the book.

The four chapters included the scene involving President Johnson in John McCormack's office. Geis said he was a little frightened about publishing something like that.

III

At about the same time I first visited Geis, I sent a chapter and outline to Dick Seaver at Grove Press. I'd done this at the suggestion of Richard Ney. And I'd promptly forgotten about it.

Seaver called me at home. It was three months since I'd sent him the outline and, until the phone call, I'd heard nothing.

The timing was good. Kittler and I didn't have to drown in our disappointment about Geis because now Seaver wanted to get together with us — with an eye to doing the book. I told him the sequence of events with Geis.

Barney Rosset, president of Grove Press, then phoned Bernie Geis to ask for confirmation of the fact that Geis didn't want to publish the book.

IV

The four of us, agents and authors, went to Grove Press to meet with Seaver. We negotiated a contract with Grove.

The Grove agreement gave us an "on signing" advance of $1,000 with another $1,500 coming, if and when Grove's lawyer, Charles (Cy) Rembar, gave Grove a "go-ahead" on the book after examining my documentation. The contract was signed December 10, 1970.

On December 17, 1970, we had our first meeting with Cy Rembar in his office. Seaver was present. Rembar's colleague, Steve Rhodie, was present. Kittler was also present at the first meeting. Kittler then told me he didn't want to "waste his time" at subsequent meetings, because the documentation had nothing to do with him.

Rembar examined a couple of hundred documents.

We had several meetings before he told Grove Press to "go ahead." These took place within a three week period.

Rembar questioned me from every conceivable angle.

"You were in McCormack's office? Describe his office. Who worked there? Describe the people." And so on.

On January 5, 1971 we received the additional $1,500. It was now "full steam ahead."

Once again we got to work. This time, at Seaver's suggestion, we dealt with subject matter rather than sequence.

Kittler and I reworked the chapter entitled "McCormack's Parlor," and turned it in to Seaver. He said it wasn't satisfactory.

In February of 1971 he wrote a letter to Toni Strassman which said in part: "— our decision has nothing to do with Mr. Kittler's professional abilities as a writer ... But, in this particular collaboration he must accurately reflect exactly, not only the context, but the very syntax of what Winter-Berger has to say. On the basis of the new material we have reviewed to date, we have come to the conclusion that the end product, that is the written material, is not an accurate reflection of the original."

At that point, we all went back to Cy Rembar's office, and there was a discussion on getting rid of Kittler. Kittler's agent was there too. Kittler and his agent refused to step aside.

Because of our inability to get out of the Kittler contract and my desire and need to get on with the book and avoid a prolonged court fight, Seaver came up with a different work method. He sent me a new Wollensack tape recorder with instructions to talk into the machine and send the tapes to Grove, who would transcribe them and send the transcription back to me. Then Kittler would meet with me and go over the forty or fifty pages to see if he had any questions. Then he'd go home and, by condensing the pages, write a finished chapter so that there was a new chapter each Thursday when we met.

This routine worked out well.

When most of the book was written, tightened, and ready to go to a typesetter, I had a new series of meetings with Cy Rembar and Steve Rhodie.

The two men went over every sentence in the manuscript. They gave me written lists of items for documentation; they wanted to substantiate item after item in each chapter.

If I couldn't furnish documentation satisfactory to the lawyers, they cut material. Occasionally, when there was heavy circumstantial evidence that I was telling the truth about something but couldn't provide a complete set of backup documents, they allowed that to remain.

The script was fine-tooth-combed.

I was constantly examined and cross-examined. Every effort was made to trip me up or to establish contradictions in what appeared in the script. Only that material which seemed absolutely unassailable was retained.

After galleys were set, the two men examined it anew. Again there were questions asked and documentation demanded.

At last they seemed satisfied.

V

A short time later, I was jolted by the bad news that Grove Press was in financial trouble. Having been deceived by their fantastic success in distributing the film *I Am Curious Yellow*, Grove had gone on a spending splurge. They bought foreign films, opened art theaters, revamped an office building and stocked it with the most expensive furniture available. When the bottom fell out, Grove found itself with large debts and no cash.

At the Frankfurt Book Fair, in the fall of 1971, Barney Rossett showed a set of unproofed galleys to Helen Meyer, president of Dell Publishing Company.

Mrs. Meyer seemed excited by the project. Where-

upon Rosset showed the script to Delacorte, a hard-
cover publishing house owned by Dell. He hoped to
sell them the clothbound rights since he wasn't able
to handle the book himself because of Grove's money
problems.

This was a mistake. We were told that their
lawyers said no: they feared libel. It was also
reported to us unofficially that an intimate member
of George Delacorte's family (he owns most of Dell)
was a patient and close friend of Dr. Arnold Hutschnecker, a psychotherapist who was not treated
lovingly in the book.

Next Grove took the script to Random House.

The Random House attorneys said no, and took
thirty-two pages in which to do it.

It was pointed out that Random House is owned by
RCA which does millions of dollars worth of business with the federal government. At a cocktail
party that took place at the St. Regis Hotel some
months later, an RCA executive told Lyle Stuart,
"The foolishness of offending senators and representatives who control large amounts of the business we do, would make it inane to distribute that
book."

Stuart, a former newspaperman, reached for a
napkin and wrote down the statement while it was
still fresh in his mind.

Both law firms came up with their negative
opinion without asking to see a single document or
proof of any statement in the script.

VI

Rosset said, "Don't worry, we'll do it ourselves. We'll find the money somewhere."

Then, suddenly, Richard Seaver resigned as editor of Grove Press to join Viking Press and launch his own line of books. This jolted me. Kittler felt he'd completed his job and was no longer working on the book and Seaver had become my only crutch.

Rosset was not discouraged. I received a phone call from him. "How would you like to have Lyle Stuart do the book?"

I said that I'd like it fine.

A meeting was arranged, and once again the two lady agents and Kittler and myself convened.

There was considerable static in the air. When I told Toni Strassman, the night before, that Stuart might become the publisher, her response had been, "Why he's worse than Geis!"

At the meeting Stuart was joined by his executive vice-president, Robert H. Salomon. Stuart seemed to know exactly what he wanted and exactly how far he would go in making the deal.

As he negated demand after demand, Toni Strassman remarked, "I have never met a publisher who could say 'no' so many times."

"Now you've had a new experience," Stuart said.

He was very sure of himself. It was obvious to me, both from his reputation and his manner, that if he did the book he'd do a good job. It was also my fear

27

that if we didn't make a deal with Stuart right on the spot, he'd walk out and not become involved. So when Kittler and both agents suggested that we "think it over," I spoke up and said, "What is this nonsense? Let's sign right now and get on with it!"

We came to an agreement. Kittler and I would take a smaller than normal share of paperback and other subsidiary rights—so that Grove Press could recoup their money and participate in profits if the book was a success.

At last we had a publisher.

A week later, when I was working on the book's index with Stuart's editor, Eileen Brand, I said, "You know, Eileen, I had the feeling that if we didn't make the deal right then and right there, Lyle would have walked out and that would have been the end of it."

She thought for a moment. "That's right," she said. "That's how he is."

CHAPTER TWO

As the production of the book went into high speed, I had meetings with the Lyle Stuart staff. The company was in the throes of planning a move in mid-March to Secaucus, New Jersey. Publication date was set for mid-April.

Kittler, who was to get dollar for dollar what I would earn on the book, now became the invisible man. He'd stopped writing the previous August. He felt his job had been done. All revisions and rewriting, and there were many, were done by myself under the heavy and expert hand of Dick Seaver until he left Grove.

At one planning conference, Lyle Stuart quietly told his people, "I'm taking the rubber band off the bankroll for this book. If any of you have any ideas on how we can break through, let me have them. I'm not just talking about space advertising. I'll do everything necessary to make an impact with this one. Its message is very important. We must not allow it to be ignored."

It was decided to employ Marc Stone to do publicity. Stone, brother of the famed journalist I. F. Stone, had been working with Grove Press and was to have handled PR for them on the book until Stuart took it over.

Stone went to Washington, D.C. He lined up interviews for me and promises of feature stories. Most of the interviews didn't appear in print, and most of the promises were eventually broken. He set up a Washington news conference for me, which was attended only by third stringers. March came and went.

In an advance announcement in *Publishers Weekly* headed: From "Lyle Stuart, Inc., the book-selling juggernaut that has become the wonder and despair of American publishing!"

—LIFE

was a full page ad which announced that 50,000 copies of my book had been printed before publication. It quoted part of the first review we received. This was from the April 1st issue of The Kirkus Service. Kirkus previews books so that bookshops, paperback editors, and libraries can know well in advance what is on the way.

Here is the review in its entirety:

> Many people — possibly a great many — will buy *and* read *The Washington Pay-Off.* Buy it because Lyle Stuart intends an advertising campaign at least equal to that lavished on *The Rich and the Super-Rich,* and read it because scattered throughout are engrossing and, in several instances, sensational disclosures concerning some of the most

recognizable names in American political life—
former President Johnson, Rhode Island Senator
Claiborne Pell, former Speaker McCormack, Congressman John Rooney, Minority Leader Gerald
Ford, President Nixon, Majority Leader Hale
Boggs—not to mention such hustling busboys of
venality as Bobby Baker, the late Nathan Volosh-
en and his side-kick Martin Sweig, and New York
Supreme Court Justice Mitchell Schweitzer. Most
of the time Winter-Berger, five years (1965-69) a
freelancing lobbyist in Washington, only extends
what we already know: there is an enormous
amount of influence-peddling and bottom-feeding
going on in Washington (e.g. compare his comment
that "GE lobbied both parties and, by Washington
rules, had the right to expect favors from whoever
was in power" with the current ITT imbroglio).

But there are certain allegations here of a more
serious personal nature in which the central issue
will surely revolve around Winter-Berger's own
credibility. His statement, for example, that a
Senator was arrested in a Greenwich Village gay
bar raid some years ago may be contested; so will
his assertion that Congressman Rooney was Voloshen's "key connection for the underworld"; and
so (perhaps) will his most incendiary tale: soon
after becoming President in 1963, LBJ, distraught
by the breaking Bobby Baker scandal, came to
then Speaker McCormack's office and said, among
other incriminating things, "John, that son of a
bitch [Baker] is going to ruin me. If that cock-
sucker talks, I'm gonna land in jail." Winter-
Berger, who claims to have been witness to this
extraordinary outburst, reports further that Johnson was crying hysterically: "I practically raised

31

that motherfucker, and now he's gonna make me the first President of the United States to spend the last days of his life behind bars."

As a lobbyist, Winter-Berger worked both sides of the aisle, for both Democrat McCormack (via Voloshen and Sweig) and Republican Ford. The amazing and ultimately incredible aspect of all of this is that Winter-Berger tries to continue the double-hat role in his book—he is privy to all of the green exchanging hands but at the same time he professes no wrongdoing: his conscience is as clean as that proverbial hound's tooth, and at one point he insinuates he was a spy among the fixers for the Justice Department.

This is an age of lying in government and hence cynicism about government. There will be those prepared to accept Winter-Berger's testimony at face value. This is the price for the failure of open government—the citizenry, denied access to the truth, its birthright, becomes a mob ready to swallow innuendo and surly rumor in lieu of full and honest information.

II

Bernard Geis now made known his desire for the return of the advance. Although I understand this is generally not done in book publishing, my agent agreed that I should refund the money. She was afraid that a lawsuit could delay publication.

Stuart was amused. "If Geis gave you an advance and then decided he didn't want to publish your book after all, the advance is yours to keep."

Since the repayment had to be an additional advance from Stuart, Barney Rosset tried to intervene. Rosset asked Stuart if he would meet with Geis for lunch.

"Only if he picks up the check," Stuart said.

Geis suggested the Gaslight Club.

"Any place but the Gaslight Club," said Stuart.

At last a time and place were fixed. The following then ensued, as reported to me by people who were there. (I wasn't.)

The place chosen was Laurent, a French restaurant in the swank Lombardy Hotel, on Manhattan's posh east side. Geis and his wife were joined by Barney Rosset. Bob Salomon and Carole Livingston of the Stuart firm sat down. Then Stuart walked into the restaurant. He was tieless.

The maitre d' took one look at the open collar and explained that Stuart would have to get a tie from the hatcheck girl.

Stuart thought for a moment and then said, "I won't do that. But I will say hello and good-bye to my friends."

He walked to the table, which was at the back and sat down.

"They won't serve us," Geis said. "The other day they refused service to a party of six because Marc Jaffe was wearing a turtle neck." (Jaffe is editor of Bantam Books, the leading paperback house.)

Stuart sat.

Finally, the captain came over and took the order.

Geis still doubted that food would be forthcoming

from the kitchen, but it was. During the luncheon Stuart said that he would make a further advance by paying Geis back the $2,500, but only because I had requested that he do so.

It was, from Geis' point of view, a successful lunch. The man who had given the world *Valley of the Dolls* and *Sex and the Single Girl* was, like Grove Press, in a financial squeeze. Probably $2,500 now seemed what $25,000 had seemed the year before.

On the way out of the restaurant, the owner stopped Geis. He was lecturing him and shaking his finger.

Stuart, amused by this, returned to the two men.

"He's giving me hell," Geis said.

"You've mortified me," said the owner to Stuart. "Nobody has ever dined here before without a necktie. You were served only because Mr. Geis is a valued customer, and we didn't want to embarrass him. Please do not ever come to this restaurant again without a necktie."

Dozens of diners at nearby tables were watching the scene. In a voice deliberately loud, Stuart replied, "I wouldn't come to this restaurant again. Your food is lousy!"

The owner's face turned a deep red as Stuart turned his back and walked out.

III

At 9:30 P.M. on the evening of April 11, 1972, I left my apartment in New York on Seventy-Fifth Street and Lexington Avenue and started to walk toward Seventy-Eighth Street for the early edition of the next morning's paper.

I had just turned the corner at Seventy-Fifth Street, when I heard a voice say, "Winter-Berger."

I turned and said, "Yes?" Suddenly I felt a hard object against my stomach, and I found myself looking at a very grim and determined expression on the face of a man I didn't know.

"Winter-Berger, this is a gun, and we're going back to your apartment," he said.

Although I had seen many gangster movies and television dramas, I never imagined that I'd be playing a role in one of them.

"Start walking," he said.

I returned to the apartment with my new companion. Once inside he directed me to show him my files.

"One at a time," he ordered.

The next hour and three quarters were an extended nightmare. I handed him file after file, and after a brief glance into each folder, he would announce angrily, "This isn't it. Get rid of it." I tossed them, one by one, onto the nearby bathroom floor.

Once I asked him to tell me what he was looking for, but this seemed to make him angrier. "You just fucking well do what you're told, and don't you ask any fucking questions, or it'll be fucking too bad with you!"

After we'd exhausted the file drawers without seeming to locate anything he wanted, he expressed some disgust and began to wander about my apartment, gun in hand. He found my gold jewelry and helped himself to it. He uncovered three hundred dollars in cash that I thought I had hidden safely from burglars.

"You got any more cash around here?"

"No," I said. "Honestly. I don't."

He stared at me for a long moment and then walked over and helped himself to my Scotch. He finished the bottle and started on my gin.

He had seemed a mean character sober, and I became frightened about how he was going to act as he drank. I talked a steady stream, and he talked too.

As if sharing a confidence, he told me that he had a "contract" for $1,000 to get some files from me. He added that he'd just spent forty-five months in prison and returning to a prison cell wouldn't bother him.

Suddenly he became disgruntled again. "Listen, Winter-Berger, you better not fuck with me. I was told this hit would be worth two grand because you would have at least a thousand in the apartment. Now, where the fuck is it?"

Again I tried to assure him that there was no other cash around. In an attempt to calm him, I said that I'd be glad to get more money but that it would take a day or two. He told me I'd better come up with another $500 quickly "or you're a dead man."

When he decided to leave, he said he was going to take me to the lobby as "hostage."

"Make all the fuss you want," he told me. "It wouldn't bother me to kill you—and the doorman too. I got nothing to lose."

I went quietly. He reminded me that he would be calling me to get the $500. He hailed a taxi and left.

Later it turned out that both the doorman and the superintendent had seen me come in with a gun at my back, and the superintendent decided that if he phoned for the police, the sirens would have frightened the intruder, and he might have killed me.

It didn't seem to occur to them that police could have been summoned and told not to use their sirens.

IV

I was in shock. How much in shock I realized only in retrospect. In a daze I walked to the newsstand at Seventy-Eighth Street and Lexington Avenue. There, from a pay phone, I called my editor, Eileen Brand, and told her what had happened. I asked if she'd agree to go to the station house with me. She agreed.

Then I got into a cab and went to her apartment on lower Fifth Avenue, several miles away.

Logic would have dictated that I go directly to the

police only a few blocks away, but I was no longer a man in full control of his thinking apparatus.

With Eileen, I went back uptown to the nineteenth precinct, at Sixty-Seventh Street between Third and Lexington Avenues.

The uniformed policeman at the desk asked me what happened.

I said that somebody held me up, forced me to take him to my apartment, and then went through my files.

"Why you?" he asked.

I was in such a trauma that I replied, "Because I wrote *The Wall Street Jungle.*"

The Wall Street Jungle was a best seller written by my friend Richard Ney and published by Grove Press. Why, in my shock, I claimed authorship of it, I'll never know. Nor did I realize that I'd so replied until Eileen told me about it once inside a detective's office, waiting to relate my story again.

The desk officer was singularly unimpressed. Nevertheless, he took me inside, and another uniformed patrolman interviewed me and took down data. I was told that the detective bureau would get in touch with me the following day.

I took Eileen back to her apartment and then returned to mine. I cleaned up the files and the other mess my uninvited visitor had made. I was shaking.

I didn't sleep very much. Every sound in the wall caused me to tense. My imagination ran wild and produced considerable fear.

The next morning I had an interview with Jim
Gash at WNEW Radio. I didn't feel up to it.

I called Lyle Stuart at his apartment. Apparently
he was just leaving.

"Listen, last night someone stuck a gun in my ribs
and made me take him to my apartment to look at
my files."

"Bob, I doubt that very much," he said casually.
"I'm off to work. Call me at the office."

I phoned Eileen. "Lyle doesn't believe me." Some-
how this shook me up almost as much as the holdup.

After Stuart got to the office, he mentioned my
call and remarked, "I don't believe it." But then he
spoke with Eileen who assured him that it had all
happened.

Meanwhile, I went to WNEW and taped ninety
minutes with Jim Gash, before going to Lyle
Stuart's office in New Jersey.

V

Two detectives, Bert Arroyo and John Sullivan,
were waiting for me when I returned to my apartment at 5:00 P.M.

They stayed with me all evening as a kind of
bodyguard. They left only when I locked my door to
go to sleep.

That evening, while they were still with me, I had
a phone call. It was the gunman. He said, "Call me

Eddie." He made a date to meet me the next day in the waiting room of Grand Central Station at 10:00 A.M. He told me to have $500 with me.

Arroyo and Sullivan arrived bright and early the next morning at 9:00 A.M.

Arroyo asked me for two one-dollar bills and then put newspaper between the bills and stuffed the resulting packet into a #6 envelope and sealed it. He gave me the envelope; it was the pay-off.

Before we left the house at 9:30 for the meeting, the detectives instructed me to take a cab to Seventy-Third Street and Lexington Avenue and have the cab wait. I did. After a few minutes the detectives arrived and got into the cab.

They got out at Forty-Third Street and Vanderbilt Avenue, and the cab continued to Forty-Second Street where I got out.

I walked into the cavernous waiting room right on the button of 10:00 A.M. I didn't see my two detectives, but I saw what seemed to be a dozen other detectives in various degrees of disguise. It certainly didn't look like just another ordinary day in the waiting room at Grand Central!

The gunman never arrived. After a half hour, I decided it was useless. I walked over to someone who looked like a detective, in a phone booth, and as I passed I said, "Tell Arroyo I'll meet him under the clock in the Biltmore."

When Arroyo came running into the Biltmore, he said, "How'd you know he was a detective? How'd you know he was one of us?"

They accompanied me to other appointments in the early afternoon. I took them to lunch, and then they watched me take a cab to the airport — for some radio and TV appearances in Boston.

When I returned two days later, I called the detectives to tell them I was back.

The thug contacted me again early the next morning. He asked me why I hadn't been at Grand Central.

"I was there," I said. "Where were you?"

He directed me to meet him at the bar of the Embassy Hotel on Manhattan's west side the following night at 1:00 A.M. He said that if he couldn't make it I should give the barmaid an envelope with $500 in it. "She'll be expecting it," he said.

I called detectives Arroyo and Sullivan again.

They picked me up the next night an hour before my designated meeting time, but now they were accompanied by a third detective. They drove to Columbus Avenue and Sixty-Ninth Street where I got out of their car.

I walked into the bar. By then it was almost one, but I didn't see Eddie. The three detectives followed separately afterwards. I ordered a drink from the barmaid, and after a few minutes I said, "I'm Bob. I'm looking for Eddie."

"Oh yes," she said. "Do you have the envelope for Eddie?"

I said, "Yes, but I don't want to give it to you. I want to give it to him personally to make sure he gets it. Do you know when Eddie is coming in?"

She called the manager over. He didn't know when "Eddie" was coming in, but he also seemed to know about the envelope. I told them I'd rather wait for Eddie. After an hour, when he didn't arrive, I left. The detectives who had wandered in after me followed me out. Arroyo and Sullivan told me to wait in their car with their colleague. Then they went back to the bar to question the manager and the girl.

The barmaid said Eddie was a friend she'd gone home with a few times and was a customer at the bar. She said he had called her earlier in the evening and told her that he wouldn't be coming in that evening and asked her to "be on the lookout" for me and keep the envelope for him. She told the detectives that he rented a room at a nearby hotel, but when they followed that up they found he'd checked out.

VI

Stuart made a statement, quoted in the press, that the police were being very ineffective. The two detectives (Arroyo and Sullivan) called to tell me that because of the adverse publicity their investigation had received, they had been called on the carpet by their superior, Lt. Edward O'Connor. They asked me to "please meet with him." I agreed. The detectives and O'Connor visited me at my apartment. Six weeks had passed since the incident.

Lieutenant O'Connor then proceeded to question me as if I was the perpetrator of the crime.

I complained in a letter to the police commissioner.

Back came an acknowledgment from Deputy Inspector William Devine. On June 12th I received a phone call from a Deputy Inspector Nicastro. We made an appointment for 10:00 A.M. at police headquarters on June 16th.

Nicastro assured me that the police had done everything they could. He apologized for O'Connor's belligerence and assured me it was "out of line," but that "he's a good man."

Nicastro was courteous and consoling. He explained that many people in the department were in awe of O'Connor at the moment because he'd just broken the Hotel Pierre Jewel Robbery Case.

That was the last I heard from the police or the gunman.

CHAPTER THREE

Trouble in the Big Apple.

Copies of *The Washington Pay-Off* had been shipped to bookshops. As is the custom, many had placed books on sale even though it was still a full month before the book's official publication day.

Now came the news that many bookshops had removed the book from sale. Rumor was that shops were being threatened. We couldn't pin it down.

Stuart's strategy had been to withhold review copies until books were actually in stores. Despite this, Rowland Evans and Robert Novak obtained page proofs of the book, and on Sunday, March 26th, their column in the *Washington Post* bore the headline "Another Mystery Book" and read as follows:

> AN EXPOSE of alleged corruption at Washington's highest levels, written by a shadowy figure describing himself as a reformed political fixer, may set off multiple denials, accusations and litigation.
>
> "The Washington Pay-Off: A Lobbyist's Own Story of Corruption in Government" by Robert N.

Winter-Berger is to be published next month by Lyle Stuart, Inc., with a first printing of 50,000. Page proofs, their existence until now unknown in political circles, have raised questions of authenticity in the New York publishing world. Thus, another mystery book has arrived.

Winter-Berger's most lurid charge is that President Johnson in 1964 asked him to relay to Johnson's beleaguered ex-lieutenant, Bobby G. Baker (now in federal prison), an offer of $1 million "if he takes this rap" without implicating anybody.

Winter-Berger also dispenses charges involving former House Speaker John McCormack and, on a considerably less sensational level, House Republican Leader Gerald Ford as well as other top political figures.

Many of these figures contacted by us professed no recollection whatever of Winter-Berger or claimed only infrequent contact with him, denying the intimacy alleged in his book. Specific incidents described by Winter-Berger drew specific denials. Accordingly, the book's authenticity boils down simply to who's telling the truth.

THE PUBLIC record indicates Winter-Berger was a fringe figure in Washington, uninvolved with great affairs of state. In the mid-1960s, he was a registered lobbyist for the now-defunct World Calendar Assn. (later renamed the Calendar Reform Management), listing payment to him of $1,000 a month. No other clients were registered.

By Winter-Berger's own account, however, his principal lobbying was to intervene with Speaker McCormack or Rep. Ford in behalf of clients having governmental troubles — in short, a fixer.

His name publicly surfaced during the 1969

45

federal influence-peddling investigation of Mc-
Cormack's lobbyist friend, the late Nathan Volosh-
en (who pleaded guilty) and McCormack's assistant, Dr. Martin Sweig (convicted of perjury). Justice Department officials told us informant Winter-
Berger was "moderately useful" but "not a major
source of information."

Winter-Berger's alleged intimacy with Volosh-
en, and through him with McCormack, leads to
accounts in the book of envelopes stuffed with cash
changing hands in return for favors. Those connec-
tions also lead to Winter-Berger's LBJ-Bobby Baker tale, seemingly incredible on its face.

On Feb. 4, 1964, writes Winter-Berger, he was in
McCormack's office when a distraught President
Johnson burst in saying, "I'm gonna land in jail" if
Baker talks. Told by McCormack that Winter-
Berger was "a close friend of Voloshen," Mr.
Johnson is quoted as giving Winter-Berger these
instructions (which Winter-Berger says he jotted
down on sheets from McCormack's personal memo
pad and still retains):

"Tell Nat (Voloshen) that I want him to get in
touch with Bobby Baker as soon as possible—
tomorrow, if he can. Tell Nat to tell Bobby that I
will give him a million dollars if he takes this rap.
Bobby must not talk. I'll see to it that he gets a
million-dollar settlement."

Winter-Berger writes that he relayed these instructions to Voloshen but does not know what was
done about them.

THE AUTHENTICITY of such material hinges on
whether Winter-Berger is what he claims. Although he writes that he and McCormack "lunched
together about twice a week for almost five years,"

the former speaker's closest associates claim no recollection of him. McCormack himself passed word to us that Winter-Berger's name "rings no bells."

Whereas Winter-Berger writes of a close relationship with Rep. Ford, the minority leader told us the lobbyist would drop by every three or four months in behalf of clients. Specific allegations in the book were described to us by Ford as "a lot of baloney," "a log of hogwash" and "ridiculous."

How did this self-described fixer get in touch with widely respected Gerry Ford? Winter-Berger claims he paid a friend of Ford $1,000 for the introduction. Telling us that Winter-Berger "did not pay me one penny," the friend intends to sue for libel. That may not be the last lawsuit generated by the strangest Washington book in many years.

More than two years have passed. The statute of limitations has expired. Not a single lawsuit has ever been filed against anyone in connection with *The Washington Pay-Off*.

II

Brentano's, Inc., submitted the book to its counselors-at-law, Ellenbogen & Klein. Stuart was asked to send Brentano's an indemnification against "liability, loss, damage or expense arising out of the sale of the book in any Brentano's store."

47

Stuart signed the indemnification.

He signed others.

It did no good.

By publication day, books had been removed from the shelves of every major bookstore in New York City. It seems that two men, working together, had written separate letters to each of the shops. The letters were sent by certified mail and threatened a lawsuit if the shop placed the book on sale.

The two were Richard H. Wels and E. Haring Chandor. Wels was an attorney who was involved in the Eddie Gilbert "fix that flopped," which I talked about in *The Washington Pay-Off*, and Chandor was Gilbert's friend and stockbroker who had gone to Wels with the Eddie Gilbert account.

The Wels letter read in part, "I am outraged by the false and defamatory statements made concerning me in this book which are of a most serious character."

I assured Stuart that every word written about Wels was true.

"That's all I want to hear from you," he said.

He got on the phone and called John T. Sargent, the president of Doubleday.

In a conversation with Sargent, he pointed out that Doubleday was a publisher as well as a bookseller, and that if a couple of threatening letters could force a book out of circulation for Stuart, similar tactics could be used against a Doubleday book in the future.

"I'll call you back," Sargent said.

One hour later the promised phone call came. "The book will go back on sale at all Doubleday shops effective immediately."

Rizzoli removed the book from its Fifth Avenue shop.

Brentano's announced that it would not handle the book despite the indemnity it had received.

William Jovanovich of Harcourt Brace Jovanovich was out of town so Stuart wrote to him. He called attention to the fact that the Harcourt Brace Jovanovich bookshop had removed the book.

Jovanovich returned. He wrote a one-line letter to Stuart. "I'm looking into *The Washington Pay-Off* matter personally and I'll let you know what I find. . ."

The next day came another one-line note. "We are putting *The Washington Pay-Off* on sale at the Harcourt Brace Jovanovich Bookstore."

Not all publishers had the courage of Sargent and Jovanovich.

Stuart spoke to Charles Scribner, Jr. He is the fourth-generation owner of the Scribner publishing company and its bookshop.

According to Stuart, Scribner evaded the issue.

"I'd like to meet with you under other circumstances," Scribner said.

"First," Stuart suggested, "why don't you have your shop put the book on sale again to show that booksellers can't be this easily terrorized? We have

nearly a million dollars in cash in the Republic
National Bank, a few city blocks from your shop.
We'll give you a solid indemnification —"

"When the case is settled —"

Stuart explained patiently, "Mr. Scribner, there is
no case to settle. Nobody has sued us. It is my feeling
that nobody will sue us. To the best of my knowledge, all the material in the book is true."

It was no use.

On the other hand, Doubleday took a forthright
positive stand. It answered Chandor's threats with a
two-page letter which said in part:

> Doubleday Book Shops serves the very impor-
> tant function of bringing books of all publishers to
> the reading public. As such, it has a responsibility
> to insure adequate distribution of the product
> while avoiding the role of censor. Upon receipt of
> your letter, contact was made with Lyle Stuart,
> Inc. in order to bring to its attention your position
> regarding the book. "The Washington Pay-Off"
> was temporarily removed from sale in our book
> shops pending advice from the publisher. Subse-
> quently, we were advised by Lyle Stuart, Inc. of its
> belief in the veracity and authenticity of the book
> and its willingness to defend its position in a court
> of law. With this assurance, "The Washington Pay-
> Off" was made available for sale in Doubleday
> Book Shops.

III

We had hoped that Brentano, Scribner's, and Rizzoli would follow this example, but they flatly refused to reverse themselves. Stuart decided that the action of the shops should be publicized.

Publishers Weekly, which prints long stories when a single book is taken from the shelves of a library in Piddle Diddle, Arkansas, totally ignored the story.

Worse, the *New York Times* ignored it.

Stuart had sent all the material to a reporter named Henry Raymont, who was covering the book industry for the *Times*.

Two weeks later Stuart let go at Raymont. In a caustic letter, he told Raymont that "This company has made considerable news of national interest in the past and will most probably do so many times again in the future. I consider you the 'idiot boy' among *Times* reporters. I am therefore putting you on notice that at no time in the future will I speak with you on any matter relating to this company or the news it makes."

He sent a copy of the letter to A. H. Rosenthal, managing editor of the *Times*, adding the paper had often published stories about book burnings and book bannings when only a single book and a small town bookshop were involved. Now major shops were being intimidated — and there wasn't a word of it in the *Times*.

Rosenthal promptly assigned Raymont to do the story.

Stuart received a phone call from him. "I told you I wouldn't talk with you ever again about any news story," Stuart said as he hung up the phone.

Two days later, a story chock full of inaccuracies appeared in the *Times* under Raymont's byline. It ended by citing my experience with the gunman but saying that the incident couldn't be confirmed by the police.

At the nineteenth precinct the police said that Raymont had never asked.

A few weeks later, Henry Raymont left the *New York Times*.

IV

A full page ad appeared in the *New York Times*.

Its headline: WHO IS TRYING TO SUPPRESS THIS BOOK?

The ad was run by the Bookmaster chain, to take advantage of the fact that not all New York City stores were stocking *The Washington Pay-Off*.

Meanwhile, Lyle Stuart, Inc., had gone public. Its 150,000 share offering was a sellout at $7.50.

Then a strange story appeared in the *Wall Street Journal*, where Dick Wels's friend, Ed Coyne, is an editor. It reported in a lead story that Wels had filed a complaint with the SEC saying that Stuart was trying to manipulate its stock by attracting publicity for *The Washington Pay-Off*.

Wels had asked the SEC to halt the sale of the stock, said the *Journal* story.

Although the *Journal* story did say that "Wels' interest in Lyle Stuart stems from some highly uncomplimentary references to Mr. Wels in 'The Washington Pay-Off,' " no reporter called Stuart for comment.

Added the story, "Nobody denies Mr. Stuart is clever at promoting books."

The story had its effect. A number of people sold their stock, fearing that maybe the SEC *would* stop it from being traded. Other people told Stuart that although they believed in him and in his company and had planned to purchase stock, they were hesitant now and preferred to see what if anything the SEC would do.

Insiders thought the SEC might take some action since Wels was once an SEC attorney.

The SEC did nothing.

Meanwhile, the stock began to fall. It eventually bottomed out at $1.50 a share.

Wels had had his revenge.

Incidentally, Stuart told me that the *Wall Street Journal* wouldn't accept an ad for the book because it was "too controversial." A *Journal* advertising man explained that the paper had turned down an ad for pregnant guppies which told the reader to "see the wonders of birth before your very eyes" because they thought the birth of small fish might be too shocking for its readers.

Since then its readers have often had to limit their shocks to the financial pages of the *Wall Street Journal* as stock prices drop and drop and drop.

V

There was no great rush to defend the book against suppression.

Media Industry Newsletter queried the American Booksellers Association on what action it would take against the concerted intimidation of its member shops.

MIN was told by ABA President Howard Klein that the organization had "no official stand on the matter. It is up to individual bookshops to act on their own. For the ABA to take any action, we'd have to have a vote of the Board of Directors and there is no precedent for that."

VI

Sometime during the previous month, Lyle Stuart wrote his first guest column for the New York-based weekly sex newspaper *Screw*. It was a clever, witty, but bawdy article.

Wels, I suspect, did not like it. Quite coincidentally, a copy of Stuart's column was anonymously sent *only* to the several people that Wels specifically knew I was friendly with. Attached to each article was this unsigned message:

"I think this will interest you.

"Despite all efforts of the establishment to suppress the truth, Lyle Stuart is now being heard.

"The attached is his first column."

One month later, Lyle Stuart wrote his next guest column for *Screw*. In it he described his problems with the bookshops that were afraid to sell *The Washington Pay-Off*.

He talked about Wels, whom he jestingly labeled Welsinski. He spoke about the sexual proclivities of Wels's wife and eldest daughter. It was very effective ridicule.

Copies were dispatched to a number of members of the Harmonie Club, a German-Jewish club with a wealthy membership. Wels is a former president of the club. Other copies were sent to Wels's friends and business associates.

It was Stuart's declaration of war against Wels.

Nothing further has ever been heard from Wels.

VII

E. Haring Chandor, who, with Wels, had succeeded in frightening the stores out of handling the book, is known as a "socialite."

A few months after the excitement, the newspapers reported that Chandor had been arrested by the FBI and charged with attempting to transport one million dollars worth of stolen IBM and Xerox stock across state lines.

The brokerage firm he worked for, Hardy & Co., quickly assured its customers that none of their stocks were involved in the stolen securities case against Chandor.

Chandor "never had access to securities in the firm's possession," a Hardy executive declared.

Chandor was seized with the stolen stock certificates at his apartment at 151 East 83rd Street in New York City.

He resigned from Hardy & Co., by mail and without explanation.

After all, what could he say?

CHAPTER FOUR

The Washington Pay-Off was beginning to make waves.

Sales passed the fifty thousand mark.

The book jumped up to sixth place on the Best Sellers list in *Time* Magazine on May 22.

Ads for the book now began to quote testimonials.

Nationally prominent attorney Melvin Belli was quoted as saying, "a fascinating and compelling exposé that names names (and they are big ones!) and dollars and dames.

"The book makes me want to march on a dirty dirty business. I hope every American will read it."

A long quote from Ferdinand Lundberg said that "... According to ex-insider Winter-Berger, there exists in the government, installed in the highest places, what amounts to a money-hungry Mafia, ready to deliver anything so long as the price is right ...

"If all the book did was to clear the way for honest men and women in politics it would be accomplishing a lot. But, being of a pessimistic nature, I fear it will only be a seasonal sensation. Grand larceny and fraud are too easily contrived under the American constitutional system."

Another ad was headlined, "If your bookseller is too frightened to supply you—use the coupon below!"

During the first week in June, the American Booksellers Association convention took place at the Shoreham Hotel in Washington, D.C.

Attending the convention, Stuart dined with a photographer who had been with the political bosses at the 1968 Republican convention.

"I was in the room," he told Stuart, "when someone came in and said that Nixon was going to select Spiro Agnew for the vice-presidential spot.

"A white-haired man who had been reading a newspaper suddenly turned around in his chair and lowered the paper. 'Nixon can't do that,' he said. 'Agnew is a thief!' "

The photographer continued, "The old man's response had been almost a reflex. Nobody said anything. A couple of fellows shrugged their shoulders and walked away. But I never forgot those words or that look on the man's face. I felt that he was speaking with the authority of certain knowledge."

Washington television stations have always been eager to present Lyle Stuart as a guest. Producers told him to let them know anytime he was in town. But now he was to be limited in what he could say. He was told he could appear only if he made no mention of *The Washington Pay-Off*.

"No way," he said.

He'd had one sour TV experience in Washington already. He'd flown down to appear on "Panorama" on the Metromedia station. They had invited him instead of me. The producer, Sheila Weidenfeld, explained that she couldn't use me because the focus would then be only on the book, but if Stuart went on, he could talk about many things, including the book.

Stuart's fellow guests were to be Prof. William Stanmeyer and attorney Melvin Belli.

Ten minutes before air time, Stuart was approached by a man in dark sunglasses who identified himself as Thomas Dougherty, a Metromedia lawyer.

"You're not to mention *The Washington Pay-Off* on this program," Dougherty said without preamble.

"Then I don't go on," Stuart said.

Dougherty backtracked. There was a hasty change of plans and instead of a live show, it was decided to tape a half-hour segment for future screening. With a tape, too much talk about my book could be edited out.

Stuart, disgusted, scarcely participated in the program.

II

Naturally I was eager for Stuart to sell paperback

rights to *The Washington Pay-Off.* He assured me that he had to play it by ear: to pick the right time and the right publisher.

Just before the ABA Convention, he told me, "I think we should limit bidding to Bantam or Dell. They're the two paperback houses who really know what they're doing."

I learned later that Bantam was cool. Its president, Oscar Dystel, just didn't believe in the genuineness of the book.

His editor, Marc Jaffe, felt otherwise. He reasoned with Dystel and pointed out that if I had been a prominent person, the exact same story would have rocked the country. But facts are facts, and the facts were there.

Dystel seemed to reverse himself.

After a lunch break, he was waiting when Stuart walked into the convention hall.

"How much do you want for that book?" he asked.

"What book?" Stuart said.

"You know what book," Dystel replied.

"Oh, *that* book!" Stuart said. He couldn't resist adding, "You don't want that book, Oscar. Why buy a book in which you only half believe?"

Thus did the bidding begin in earnest.

It ended the next morning when Stuart sat with Dell executives on the terrace overlooking the Shoreham Hotel gardens. Rights were sold for a guaranteed advance of $150,000 plus $25,000 in advertising money.

We were off and running.

CHAPTER FIVE

It wasn't all caviar and champagne.

That week, Stuart's attorney Jack N. Albert wrote to John Leonard, editor of the *New York Times* Sunday book section.

> For many years, our client has felt that the preparer of your "Best-Seller" list arbitrarily discriminates against it. As only one of the many examples, when "The Sensuous Man" had already sold over one quarter of a million copies, your list had it in second place, while the first place book did not have more than 100,000 copies in print.
>
> We feel that a serious situation now exists with regard to the captioned book [*The Washington Pay-Off*]. While we recognize the existence of a time lag in your list, "The Washington Pay-Off" has been on *Time* Magazine's list for five weeks (fourth place, two weeks ago); it is in *Publishers Weekly's* list and it was in fifth place on the Newsday list, last week, as well as on other lists of leading sellers. More than 50,000 copies of "The Washington Pay-Off" have been sold within a six week period which sales record easily exceeds the total sale of at least four of the ten books on your current list.

The *New York Times* totally ignored the book, both on its daily book page and in its Sunday Book Section.

Nor did *The Washington Pay-Off* ever appear on the best seller list of the *New York Times*.

II

We did receive some review space.

Brit Hume, then an associate of Jack Anderson, wrote an enthusiastic review which was front-paged in *Book World* — a Sunday supplement in the *Washington Post*.

Playboy wrote:

> If one is to believe former lobbyist Robert N. Winter-Berger, venality among Government officials and the lower judiciary is more rampant than even Jack Anderson could imagine. By way of profitable penance for his own role in the brothel of public affairs, Winter-Berger has written *The Washington Pay-Off* (Lyle Stuart). Presumably, the publisher has excellent libel lawyers.
>
> Among those accused by Winter-Berger of engaging in a diversity of sleazy practices are Richard Nixon, Lyndon Johnson, the late Sam Rayburn, former House Speaker John McCormack, former Supreme Court Justice Tom Clark (when he was U. S. Attorney General), House Minority Leader Gerald Ford, and a host of others — in Congress, in the military-industrial complex, wherever the right official word can provide some

people with more equal protection of the laws than others.

A large part of the book is devoted to the intricate affairs of the late master fixer, Nathan Voloshen, with whom the author was associated and on whom he eventually spied for the Government. In detailing Voloshen's enveloping web of influence — from Capitol Hill to the suzerains of the underworld — Winter-Berger has constructed a classic case history of the kind of subversion of democratic government that is far more destructive than any conspiracies by revolutionaries. An intriguing motif throughout the book is the author's charge that even when corruption is exposed, the authorities (of whatever political party) often succeed in cutting off an investigation before it gets to the highest levels of Governmental involvement. Some of the material in this handbook of illicit influence is familiar — the selling of ambassadorships, the incestuous relationship between the Defense Department and some of its contractors and suppliers. But Winter-Berger does give specifics: names, dates and even, on occasion, incriminating dialog.

As for reform, the author sees no hope for its coming from within our Governmental institutions. Only a probing press and an aroused citizenry can purge our official agencies of corruption. Meantime, the payoffs go on.

Gore Vidal, writing in the *New York Review of Books* praised the book with enthusiasm. His review said in part:

It is no wonder that most newspapers and magazines have refused to review this book and that many bookstores will not sell it. The fear is not of libel. Something much more elemental is involved. If the corruption and greed of the men the Property Party has placed in the Congress and the White House become common knowledge, the whole rotten business could very well collapse and property itself would be endangered.

Had there actually been a two-party system in the United States, the incoming President would have taken advantage of such an extraordinary scandal in the Democratic ranks. Instead, Nixon moved swiftly to remove Robert Morgenthau from office.

If there is one thing Nixon understands, it is dominoes. Or as Mr. Winter-Berger puts it, "at the time, Voloshen said to me: 'Mitchell is afraid that if any of the Congressmen are found guilty, the whole public image of the Congress would be destroyed.' Voloshen also told me about the proviso which Attorney General Mitchell added to his offer to drop the case against Frenkil (Voloshen's pal): House Speaker John McCormack would have to resign from Congress. Knowing how much Mc-Cormack loved his job and his life in the world of politics, I didn't think such a powerful man would go along. But in fact he did."

But elsewhere there was still the blackout problem. Instead of burdening the reader with every example, allow me to cite two. I mentioned earlier that on the morning after the gun was stuck against my stomach, I taped one and a half hours for the Jim Gash Show on WNEW Radio.

WNEW is a Metromedia station. Gash was told he couldn't use the tape. Mark Evans, Metromedia's Washington lobbyist, did not want me to appear on any of their stations. He said that my appearance could anger the Federal Communications Commission and endanger the license renewals for Metromedia stations. Gash said he would resign. A compromise was reached, and from time to time, Gash was permitted to play small snatches of the interview.

Case two: Gil Noble is a good-looking, bright, smooth-talking commentator on ABC-TV in New York. He happens to be black.

He became quite excited about the book.

He interviewed me for three-quarters of an hour. He brought a TV crew of three to make a television tape of the interview.

Then he took the crew and equipment to Lyle Stuart's mid-Manhattan apartment and spent an hour with him. Both Stuart and I told it like it was, and Noble was fascinated.

"This is hot stuff!" he said when he departed.

The hot stuff was too hot for Channel Seven to handle. It was put on ice. Nothing. Not a peep about the book. Not two seconds from either interview.

When the Watergate scandals broke, Noble tried again. He felt with certainty that now the powers who censor such things would realize that there was something more than fairy tales in *The Washington Pay-Off.*

Noble's noble intentions were for nought.
Nothing on Channel Seven.

III

MORE is a journalism review that is highly respected by newsmen everywhere. It has guts and style.

Brit Hume did an investigative piece on the book and our problems. He checked out all of Stuart's charges against the media.

He noted that a Miss Alice Weston had said she would sue for libel. But she hadn't sued.

I met Alice Weston when we both worked for a small public relations agency. Weston was her professional name, her legal name being Mrs. Arthur Schowalter.

She mentioned to me that her family was very close to Gerald Ford. She brought this up because she knew of my close relationship with John Mc-Cormack.

I let her know that I wasn't happy with the way things were being handled from McCormack's office and that I'd like to meet Rep. Gerald Ford.

She said she could arrange it.

Privately, I thought she was bragging, and so I didn't push the matter. But when she mentioned it again and again over a period of months, I decided to call her bluff.

I asked if it were really true that her father had

helped Ford get his start and that her brother, Peter
Boter, was close to him, and she said yes.

I asked if her brother could write a letter of
introduction to Ford for me.

She said she was sure she could get her brother to
write such a letter. However, she said that her
brother, who had a very protective attitude towards
her, wouldn't want her to do it without some
remuneration.

"Fine. How much would he expect you to get for
this introduction?"

"I don't think he would set any price on it. You
know that I'm a working girl —"

"How much do you want?" I asked.

"A thousand dollars."

"You must be kidding!" I explained that it was too
much money. I might only meet him once. What I
wanted, I explained, was to get to know him so I
could work with his office as I did with Mc-
Cormack's.

"Let's try it this way," she suggested. "Five
hundred dollars for the introduction and five
hundred dollars if it takes."

I agreed.

She said she wanted the money in cash.

Again, I agreed.

The letter was written on April 19, 1966. I was
now her client. She went to Washington with me,
and we met with Ford during the last week in May
of 1966.

I paid her the first $500 in July of 1966. She'd

LOKKER, BOTER & DALMAN
ATTORNEYS AT LAW
PEOPLES STATE BANK BUILDING
HOLLAND, MICHIGAN 49423

CLARENCE A. LOKKER
PETER S. BOTER
RONALD L. DALMAN

TELEPHONE
EXport 2-937
AREA CODE 61

April 19, 1966

Honorable Gerald R. Ford
Member of Contress
Rayburn Building
Washington, D. C.

Dear Jerry:

My sister, Alice Weston, is at the present time engaged in
public relations work in New York City. She has a client,
Robert N. Winter-Berger, who has expressed a desire to meet
you and discuss some matters with you. I have suggested to
her that she call you and identify herself as my sister, and
indicated that if it were at all possible I was sure that you would
give her such time as you might have available. I know that
with your added duties as the Minority Leader, you must have
an extremely busy schedule. However, I would appreciate anything which you could do to be of assistance to her.

We are all most interested in the developing Senatorial contest.
While I hope that Bob Griffin makes it, I am also hopeful that
his opponent will be one other than G. Mennen Williams.

With kindest personal regards, I remain

Very truly yours,

psb:em

been pressuring me for her payment, but I didn't have the money.

I paid her the second $500, also in cash, about a month later.

Subsequently, she was to deny that I ever paid her anything or even that I paid her expenses. Fortunately, as will be seen, I did have documents to show her a liar.

Hume also pointed out that the column by Rowland Evans and Robert Novak had appeared in the *Washington Post,* but the *New York Post* had killed it.

He wrote: "Except for Stuart's ads and the book's visibility in store windows, it seems as if *The Washington Pay-off* was never published. Columnists Evans and Novak's expectation of lawsuits and their suspicion of the book's credibility have been shared by virtually the entire Washington press corps and the book editors of nearly every major magazine, newspaper and network."

Hume checked with Charles Rembar whom he quoted as saying that I had been given "10 to 15 hours of hostile cross-examination that an author might expect from an opposing attorney in a libel suit."

Rembar also said, "I thought his story hung together very well."

Howard Manges, a veteran publisher's lawyer, explained Random House's decision not to distribute the book for Grove Press.

"We think," said Manges, "that the book contains certain material that would tend to demonstrate the unreliability of the author."

When pressed, he explained that "the author was present at several acts of crime and kept silent about them."

Did the firm ever contact me before making up its mind about my credibility?

"We never had a conference with him," Manges told Hume. "Documentation was never offered us, and we never demanded it."

Jack Anderson was censored by Metromedia when he attempted to broadcast an item which said that, based on his own earlier reporting, he could vouch for much of what I had written.

Hume ended by citing a typical case, that of Shelby Coffey, III.

Coffey was the newly appointed editor of the *Washington Post*'s Sunday *Potomac* magazine.

"His attitude," wrote Hume, "is symbolic of the attitude of the press in general. He asked Washington freelance writer, Robert Sherrill, to check out Stuart's ads to see if they were fraudulent. Sherrill's checking revealed, however, that Stuart's assertions about the book's difficulties were true. Coffey said part of the reason for not then pursuing the matter further was that he knew a review was coming out in the *Post*'s book section. He acknowledged, however, that his main interest had been in catching Stuart with a hoked-up ad rather than catching the book industry suppressing *The Washington Pay-Off.*"

IV

The ad campaign for the book continued.

In some papers, full page ads carried the bold headline:

Johnson, Nixon and Jezibel Jones—
Who got the graft and who got the loans?

Other papers felt that headline too strong, and so it was toned down to:

Johnson, Nixon and other Big Names
—All in the book including the dames!

What I enjoyed best about them, however, was the first paragraph which reported, "Despite desperate attempts to suppress this book, nearly 70,000 copies have been sold in seven weeks!"

And it was going for $10 a copy!

CHAPTER SIX

In 1972, there were 26,868 new books published in the United States. That meant that on every weekday, an average of more than one hundred new titles made their appearance and were competing for attention. One hundred new books each and every day. Most remain unheard of, even by most of their author's acquaintances. Those few that attain fame are in the spotlight only a brief moment and then are forgotten as the tidal wave of new titles pushes them into oblivion.

Books come and go. *The Washington Pay-Off* had its time in the spotlight. And then the spotlight turned to other faces and other places.

There was no sex per se in *The Washington Pay-Off*. I wasn't telling people how to double their money in the stock market overnight. Or how to lose twenty pounds a week or make love four times a day or breed milk goats.

And so, as the days rolled into weeks and the weeks pyramided into months, the book lost its display space in those windows where shopkeepers were courageous enough to show it. It dropped from best seller lists.

Stuart decided that Dell should cash in on his abundant and expensive advertising. He therefore waived the usual one year waiting period and allowed a Dell paperback to appear.

The cloth edition was $10, and the Dell edition was $1.75. Stuart remarked to me that he would have preferred a $1.50 price.

"I may be wrong but I think Dell is mistaken. They're trying to recoup their large advance by a large price. They'd have a better shot at it if they kept the price to $1.50. I'll bet they'd increase sales 20 percent or more."

But what was done was done.

The paperback appeared in October, 1972, deliberately timed for preelection sales.

What nobody had anticipated was that the 1972 presidential election was destined to be one of the dullest in American history.

The people who yearned for a father figure or a hero, settled instead for Richard Nixon. They refused to place their faith in Senator George McGovern — the man who seemed to be the most indecisive Hamlet in political history. From day to day and from hour to hour he'd vacillate. He'd take a position, reverse it, do a half gainer, and then fall flat on his face.

Jack Benny would undoubtedly have run up a larger vote for the Democrats.

Net result: an immediate sale of about 200,000 paperback copies.

Not bad but not what many felt the book deserved.

In his own haste to publish, Stuart settled for the dust jacket that Grove Press had prepared for itself. Dell then picked up the same jacket. In retrospect, perhaps something more nearly directed at the paperback-buying audience would have helped.

But the earth turned and I had had my moment in the sun.

And at that moment, "Watergate" was, to most people who knew of its existence, merely an apartment house complex in Washington, D.C.

II

London's *New Statesman* is an internationally respected journal. It is read by opinion makers and decision makers throughout the world.

It was therefore gratifying to learn that *The Washington Pay-Off* wasn't completely forgotten.

On May 4, 1973, *New Statesman* carried an article about Washington, D.C. politics by Gore Vidal.

Vidal wrote:

> Last year a remarkable book was published in the United States, "Washington Pay-Off" by Robert N. Winter-Berger. At first hand, the author, a former lobbyist, described how the Speaker of the House of Representatives, John McCormack, rented space in his Capitol office to a master criminal named Nathan Voloshen. From the Speaker's office

a team of influence peddlers sold favours to innumerable clients. Eventually they were busted by U.S. Attorney Robert Morgenthau. Voloshen went to jail. The Speaker was persuaded to retire from Congress. This horror story was one of several carefully detailed by Mr. Winter-Berger: each involved some of our most celebrated public men.

Needless to say, the book did not please the owners of the United States, a loose consortium that includes the editors of the *New York Times* and the *Washington Post*, the television magnates, the Rockefellers, Kennedys, ITT, IBM, etc. Winter-Berger's exposes were largely ignored by the press and television. The book did become a best seller but never became what it should have been, a subject for national debate. Intrigued by the silence the book had aroused, I rang Robert Morgenthau and asked him if he thought Winter-Berger a reliable witness in the high Whittaker Chambers sense of the word. Morgenthau said that, all in all, the text was accurate.

He then quoted passages from the book.

Ego but not sales were boosted. The clothbound edition was scarce, and the paperback had virtually disappeared from the newsstands.

For all practical purposes, *The Washington Pay-Off* was dead and forgotten.

Book Two

Two statements worth repeating . . .

1. "I scarcely know Robert N. Winter-Berger. I may have met him eight or ten times. I may have written to him five or six times."

Gerald Rudolph Ford

2. "I sometimes saw Jerry Ford as often as seven or eight times a month—over a three and a half year period. A lobbyist's job is most often done verbally with the legislator who is doing him a favor. As little as possible is put in writing, for the obvious reason. Even so, Jerry Ford wrote to me and my clients some fifty times."

Robert N. Winter-Berger

Conclusion that requires no great IQ:
   One of us was lying.

KALEIDOSCOPE

In 1973 in the United States of America, you could hardly follow the game without a scorecard.

On August 6, the Vice President of the United States, Spiro Agnew, announced that he was under investigation for extortion, bribery, and tax evasion.

"It's all untrue," he insisted. "I am innocent."

Two days later he added that reports that he took kickbacks from contractors in Maryland were "damned lies." He said further, "I repeat that I have no expectation of being indicted and no intention of resigning from office. I am innocent."

On August 15, Agnew agreed, for the first time, to answer personally a series of questions posed by U.S. Atty. George Beall and to open his records to Beall. Beall was investigating the many charges against Agnew. The vice president again announced, "I am innocent."

On August 21, Agnew denounced the Justice Department for its effort to indict him. "I will fight to preserve my innocence. I am innocent!"

On September 29, in a speech before Republican clubwomen in California, Vice President Agnew declared, "I will not resign if indicted." Again he said, "I am innocent."

On October 10, "innocent" Spiro Agnew, who said he would never resign, resigned from office. He pleaded nolo contendere (no contest) to a $29,000 tax evasion for bribes received when he was governor of Maryland.

In return for his plea, Attorney General Elliot Richardson asked Judge Walter E. Hoffman to forgo putting Agnew in jail. Hoffman sentenced Agnew to three years in prison but suspended the sentence. He also fined Agnew $10,000.

Judge Hoffman announced that "I would have sent him to jail under ordinary circumstances, if Attorney General Richardson had not interceded."

In the corridor, outside the courtroom, Spiro Agnew again told news reporters, "I am innocent."

II

That day, President Richard M. Nixon sent a letter to his former vice-president.

"Dear Ted," it began. It went on to praise the convicted felon for his "courage and candor" and praised him for his "patriotism and dedication."

The president expressed his "great sense of personal loss."

The U.S. attorney general's office later revealed that it had gathered evidence to show that Agnew asked for and received bribes totaling more than $100,000 while in three elective public offices including that of the vice-presidency of the United States.

(The president had not yet made the now-famous statement about his own innocence in which he declared flatly, "I am not a crook!")

III

The president of the United States refused to respond to subpoenas for tapes until he was on the brink of being cited for contempt of court. Then he produced seven instead of nine, saying that two didn't exist.

On October 20th, President Nixon ordered Attorney General Richardson to fire Watergate Special Prosecutor Archibald Cox. He refused and resigned. His deputy, William D. Ruckelshaus, was fired when he also refused to fire Cox. The president got his way when he appointed Richard H. Bork as acting attorney general, and he agreed to dismiss Cox.

One month later, an embarrassed White House attorney told the court that eighteen minutes of a tape had been erased. This was a critical section, and one in which the president's discussion with his then chief of staff, H. R. Haldeman, could have given the lie to Nixon's statement that he knew nothing of Watergate or the Watergate cover-up.

The things that were now being exposed nationally were like bad playbacks of things I had described in my book.

Four hundred and twenty thousand dollars collected as "Nixon campaign contributions" were distributed covertly to the seven Watergate defendants, their families, and their lawyers.

Another bombshell: Shortly before the case against Daniel Ellsberg was to go before the jury, President Nixon had sent White House aide John Ehrlichman to the judge to find out whether he might like to be appointed director of the FBI.

The judge, William Matthew Bryne, Jr., expressed anger at what he considered a blatant attempt to influence him. He later dismissed all charges against Ellsberg "with prejudice."

Erle Stanley Gardner could have gotten two complete mysteries out of the daily headlines. *The Case of the Missing Tapes* and *The Case of the Erased Tapes.*

On November 12, 1973, *Time* published its first editorial in fifty years. It called for the resignation of Richard Nixon.

"Richard Nixon and the nation have passed a tragic point of no return. It now seems likely that the President will have to give up his office: he has irredeemably lost his moral authority, the confidence of most of the country, and therefore his ability to govern effectively.

". . . The catalog of the President's involvement in illegal or grossly improper acts has become all too familiar . . ."

CHAPTER ONE

There is a story told in Hollywood that when film mogul Jack Warner heard that Ronald Reagan was going to run for the governorship of California, he is reported to have blurted out: "No! No! Fred Mac-Murray for governor. Ronald Reagan as best man."

That's a little bit of how I felt when I heard that Richard Nixon was going to nominate Gerald Ford to fill the vice-presidential vacancy.

"That's like Al Capone picking Stan Laurel as his successor," I thought to myself.

II

Immediately after Spiro Agnew resigned on October 10th, House Speaker Carl Albert phoned the White House and persuaded the president that Gerald Ford "would be the easiest candidate to sell to the House."

The recommendation was not made on the basis of Ford's talent or experience. His qualifications were minimal.

The heat was on Nixon to resign. Probably no

president in American history had so brazenly lied to the people, had so misused executive power, or had engaged in so much criminal activity and lawlessness.

Carl Albert's reputation wasn't all that snow white either. In *The Washington Pay-Off* I described Albert's close friendship and business dealings with Nathan Voloshen. Voloshen was the well-known influence peddler who introduced me to Washington. I described his involvement in the meeting with Victor Frenkil, a Baltimore contractor who tried to collect five million dollars in excess charges for building the garage of the Rayburn House Office Building. Voloshen convened a meeting of "the boys" in Congress among whom were Albert and John McCormack.

Those present assured Frenkil in different ways that he had "nothing to worry about."

Albert knew Nixon's problem in much the same way that a corrupt cop in Chicago can sympathize with a corrupt cop in Newark, New Jersey, when the latter faces serious charges.

III

At that point, President Nixon obviously planned to brazen out all the cries for his impeachment. He needed to take some of the hostility out of the House of Representatives. One obvious way to do this was to select "one of their own" as VP.

After more than a quarter of a century in Congress, Gerald Ford would have to be a mute cretin if he couldn't control the votes of a few dozen members of the House. The back-slapping, joke-telling, hail-fellow camaraderie of the House membership would stand Ford and Nixon in good stead.

Richard Lyons, writing in the *Los Angeles Times*, commented that "The smart guys said that Ford was a good-looking Boy Scout needed to give Republicans a better television image."

The Newhouse News Service explained in its newspapers that "By nominating House Republican Leader Gerald R. Ford of Michigan to be his new vice-president, President Nixon is continuing to gather around him men who have influence with Congress . . . [Ford] no doubt, has accumulated a pocketful of I.O.U.'s for favors done in the past."

The *Wall Street Journal* headlined the story of the nomination by describing Ford as "No Intellectual Heavyweight." It described his record as that of a Nixon flunky and "a tireless advocate of any and all Nixon causes." It labeled him a hard-working but "plodding" man.

Republican National Chairman George Bush announced that he thought President Nixon did the "smart" thing in nominating Ford. He said this between tennis matches with Spiro Agnew, a month after the former vice-president had resigned "disgraced" but with only a slap on the wrist by the courts.

CHAPTER TWO

I always liked Jerry Ford. I still like him. Unlike many of the other congressmen that I knew and worked with and bought, Ford had his fingers on everything that was going on in his office. It had the atmosphere of a public library with everyone talking in whispers. Very little authority was delegated, and Ford's was one office that operated at maximum efficiency.

For me to get something done in Speaker John McCormack's office, I only had to speak to Martin Sweig. In Ford's office, there was only one person to talk to: Gerald Ford. It was Ford himself and only Ford who decided what favors were to be parceled out.

We hit it off almost immediately after the first meeting that I described in *The Washington Pay-Off.*

Even before I asked Jerry for a favor, I offered to do a favor for him. I offered to help him write a speech.

He gave me a rough draft that he said had been typed by his wife at home. He specifically told me not to mention the matter to Paul Miltich, his press representative.

The speech was headed: "Now is the hour . . ."

I took his outline and rewrote it for him.

He delivered the speech on June 11, 1966 at Parsons College in Iowa.

It was a demagogic talk. In part it warned against beginning a friendship with Communist China, an attitude contrary to Nixon's later position.

The speech was not terribly deep. But then Jerry Ford is not terribly deep. It was full of slogans and calls for patriotism. The speech said nothing but it said it well. It was one of those typical political vaudeville acts where the magician saws the lady in half, and you know he's not really doing a thing except creating a wispy illusion.

Nevertheless, Ford was pleased. He made very few alterations.

I had begun to ingratiate myself with him.

And that, dear reader, is what lobbying is all about.

II

As I said, I liked Jerry Ford. But, as Senator Gaylord Nelson of Wisconsin remarked when voting against Senate confirmation of Ford for the vice-presidential post, "We are, after all, selecting a potential president . . . I don't believe that he can provide the kind of leadership that this nation desperately needs."

Jerry is an easygoing fellow.

When I first met him he was humble and unsure of himself.

And when I first met him he became, for me, a hero figure.

Here at last, I thought, is a congressman who isn't on the take. I may win his favor with things like speech writing, but I will not be able to buy his favor with money.

At least, that's the way it seemed to me then.

III

In 1966 Jerry Ford was so unsure of himself that he asked me whether he should deliver a speech in another city or attend a White House briefing.

He asked me where I got my shirts and ties and suits. He wanted to know if I could get clothes for him wholesale.

He knew very little and made no pretense of knowing much.

He had just become minority leader of the House of Representatives.

It took about a year for him to change. As he realized the power he had, he became arrogant and opinionated. He no longer asked for advice: he issued directives.

87

From 1966 to 1969 I observed a complete meta-morphosis.

He developed from a man unsure of himself to a man who "knew all the answers."

The only problem was that he didn't know any more in 1969 then he knew in 1966.

Fortune magazine said in March, 1974, that "If some writer tried to put together a book entitled *The Wit and Wisdom of Gerald Ford*, it would have to be a pretty slim volume, even with large type and thick paper. Still, no one should assume from Ford's lack of brilliance that he is the muttonhead L.B.J. tried to make him out to be ..."

The magazine was referring to the late President Johnson's remarks that "Too bad Jerry played so much football with his helmet off," and "Jerry is the only man I ever knew who can't chew gum and walk at the same time."

Ford was a constant butt of jokes about his mediocre mind, lack of imagination, and miniature vision. Larry King, wrote in the magazine *New Times*:

When Mel Laird was House Minority Whip (his boss was House Minority Leader Gerald Ford) ... a story circulated on Capitol Hill that Laird, seeking votes for a Republican bill, was asked if his understanding of that bill coincided with Jerry Ford's. Laird is alleged to have responded, "I haven't had time to explain it to him."

The story enjoyed wide Capitol Hill circulation;

few insiders hearing it failed to laugh in appreciation of its presumed tidy truth.

What is "truth"?

James Reston has written, "Mr. Ford had demon-
strated that he is not very smart, but that he is
honest."

Gerald Ford has helped to spread the "honest
Gerald Ford" myth by saying over and over again
that "a president should be truthful."

This is "honest Jerry" who, in 1968, bought new
clothes to wear on the rostrum of the Republican
Convention and then tried to deduct their cost on his
income tax.

This is "honest Jerry Ford" who in 1972 collected
$100,000 in campaign contributions. Gifts of $500 or
more came from fifteen people, only two of whom
lived in Ford's congressional district. Jerry received
$4,000 from the Associated Milk Producers whose
contribution to President Nixon is, at this writing,
under investigation by the special Watergate prosecutor and the Senate Watergate committee.

Incidentally, where Jerry had $100,000 to spend,
his opponent could only raise $10,000.

Ford has always been supported by what we know
as "big business."

He has been little more than "a nice guy" and a
devoted congressional clerk who thought small,
when he thought at all. Ford's name appears on no
important piece of legislation although he served in
Congress for a quarter of a century.

"Nobody," said *Fortune*, "could call Gerald Ford 'antibusiness.' The chief Washington lobbyists for Ford Motor Co. and U.S. Steel are among his closest personal friends."

So was I.

V

During the early weeks of our relationship, Jerry and I had developed a warm rapport.

Then, about six weeks after we met, I wanted him to endorse "The World Calendar." This was a crusade by the late Elisabeth Achelis, a wealthy eccentric multimillionaire who lived in New York, and for the last forty years of her life, had campaigned for calendar reform, in the name of her own dream the World Calendar.

This is a standardized calendar where there would be thirteen months to the year, and every year would begin on Sunday, January 1.

Miss Achelis inherited her fortune from the Ace Comb Company and the Commercial Factor Corporation. She was eighty-five or eighty-six years old when I met her for the first time. She promptly hired me and agreed to pay me a fee of $1,000 a month plus expenses.

Jerry thought the World Calendar a crackpot scheme being promoted by a crackpot spinster, and, at first, he declined to become involved.

After failing to change his mind twice, I hit upon

90

a new approach. I could use Miss Achelis's money to do a Nathan Voloshen. Voloshen had taught me that the quickest and surest way to get a politician to do anything was to pay him off by making a "campaign contribution" in the form of "just plain cash."

In the middle of July, 1966, I went to Ford's office, closed the door, sat across from him, and placed a white envelope on his desk that contained $2,000 in large bills. I was doing just what I had seen Voloshen do with others.

"Here's something for you," I said.

Jerry didn't touch the envelope. He didn't even seem curious about what was in it. He looked at it and then put his hand out, symbolically brushing it away.

"No, Bob," he said. "That's not how I do business. If you want to, you'll have plenty of time to make campaign contributions. Right now it's the summer, and we haven't gotten started yet."

I told him that I needed some sort of endorsement from both sides of the aisle of Congress in order for me to get an article in any of the major newspapers.

"Well, we'll see about it," he said.

It took another month before he would dictate a brief statement to his secretary, Mildred Leonard. He corrected it with his own pen.

About four weeks after that, thanks to Ford's statement and to one the *New York Times* now had from Senator John Pastore of Rhode Island, it published an article.

Calendar reform has long been sought by many responsible individuals worldwide.

For obvious reasons in our now more complicated industrial world the arguments for such a change may be more persuasive. In the past Members of Congress, including the late Estes Kefauver who favored the world calendar, have sponsored legislation in this area. As one looks at the future it might be wise for the Congress to take a look at the increasing problems and the need for calendar reform.

92

The article appeared opposite the editorial page on September 26, 1966. It pleased Miss Achelis very much.

I described my first campaign contribution in *The Washington Pay-Off* as follows:

It was during Ford's campaign for re-election that I found out how close he was to Richard Nixon. At the time, I had known Jerry for about five months. On Wednesday, September 21, 1966, I was in his office around ten-thirty in the morning and, in the course of a general conversation, I mentioned to him that Jack Slater, who was the fundraising head of the Republican Party in the Detroit area, had approached me for a contribution from my friends, and I asked: "Jerry, would it be helpful to you if I contributed something?"

"It would be nice of you if you did," he said. "But now that you've mentioned it, I'm having fundraising dinner in Grand Rapids on October 25, and it would be more important to me if you contributed to that. How about taking five tickets?"

"How much are they?"

"A hundred apiece."

"Okay."

"Swell."

On Monday, October 17, I delivered my check made out to the Kent County Republican Committee, for these tickets personally to Jerry. He was delighted. He said: "I hope you'll be there, Bob. I don't want to look at the same old faces."

I assured him I would. I knew that many lobbyists bought tickets to such events because they knew they had to, but most often they gave the tickets to the politician's staff so that they could attend the event in a show of devoted loyalty that wasn't costing them anything. But I already had a lot riding on Jerry Ford, and I was determined to attend the dinner even if I had to walk to Grand Rapids. Actually, I flew to Detroit where a friend of mine met me and drove me to Grand Rapids. With us at the dinner that night at the Grand Rapids armory were Alice Weston, to whom I had originally paid the $1,000 for the introduction to Ford, and her brother, Peter Boter, who had written Ford the letter which had led to the introduction.

There were about 800 people at the banquet, and the star was Richard Nixon. Ever with his eye on the White House, Nixon rarely missed a chance to appear at a Republican event, keeping his name in people's minds and picking up the indebted loyalty of candidates he was helping by his appearance. Nixon didn't have to worry about Ford's loyalty. In the short time I had known him, Ford had assured me many times that he and Nixon were close friends. This was borne out by the speeches. Nixon told the audience that Ford was going to be the next Speaker of the House of Representatives. Ford told the audience that Nixon was going to be the next President of the United States. In the middle of his speech, Ford startled me by turning in my direction and saying: "And I want to thank my good friend Bob Winter-Berger for coming all the way out here from New York for this dinner." There was an uncertain sprinkle of applause. Nobody knew who I was, which, as a lobbyist, was the way I wanted it.

VI

The first cash exchanged hands in July, 1966.

Having struck out with Ford once, I asked Nat Voloshen for advice. "Try again. There isn't anyone I know who doesn't need cash. It's all in the timing."

The next time I was alone with Jerry in his office, he asked me how the old lady was coming along. He knew that at that point she was my only client.

Then he mentioned to me a problem he was having with one of his sons. He went into a monologue about all of the expenses of raising four children.

I said, "Jerry, you know I don't have much money to give, but I'll be happy to lend you a couple of hundred."

He replied, "No, Bob, that won't be necessary. You can't afford that sort of thing."

"Well, let me see," I said. I took out my wallet and counted out $200. I held them out and he took them.

"I'm most appreciative, Bob," Ford said, putting the money away. I can't recall now whether he put it in his pocket (which he did sometimes in the many times that followed) or slipped it into his desk (which he did at other times). In either case, the money quickly vanished from sight.

I left the office. I felt elated. I felt that I had scored. Voloshen had always insisted that money was the key to every politician's heart.

95

VII

Ten days later. In the intervening period I'd dropped in to see Jerry two or three times, "just to keep the fire of friendship warm."

Now, as I sat and listened, I became aware that Jerry was talking about his problems again.

I should make clear to the reader that as minority leader of the House in the summer of 1966, he had to concern himself with the problems of the 187 Republican members of Congress. Thus, the procedure, when I wanted to see him, was to tell Mildred Leonard, "I just want five minutes."

The understanding was always that one was expected to be in and out of his office in five or ten minutes.

So, when I found him talking about his own problems, I knew that the situation was a little abnormal. I couldn't bolt for the door while he was describing his mother's illness, problems with his children (one of his three sons "wasn't serious enough"), problems about his wife complaining that she didn't see enough of him and of her ailments and other complaints.

Again he was telling me how much it costs to raise children.

I gave him another small contribution.

"This is a personal loan," he said. "It has nothing to do with campaign contributions."

Once on doing me a favor he had stated, "I'd do it for you anyway, Bob. Your loans have nothing to do with it."

VIII

Lyle Stuart warned me when I began this book that I had better level with you all the way.

I have been asked why I kept no record of the "loans."

The fact is that although we talked about "loans," I felt very uncertain about the legality of the transaction. The money exchange was always so private and with so much seeming "understanding" between the two of us that I hesitated to even think the thing through. All I knew was that I was pleased to be very close to the minority leader of the House of Representatives. All I hoped for was that I would make the right contact and find someone who would pay well for my inside track. I felt strongly that given any reasonable request, Jerry would not turn me down. He was, in a kind of way, on my pad . . .

At that time I felt flush. The small amounts (never more than $250 at a time and never less than $50) meant little to me.

Three months after I began to work for her, Elisabeth Achelis told me in a letter that she'd paid me $6,700 in "expenses." That was more than $2,000 a month. It was in addition to my fee of $1,000 a month.

(Two weeks before she had written to me in her own hand, "I do not wish to restrict you, but we cannot afford to be lavish. Travel expenses are necessary, but plan to reduce, if possible, and guard against unnecessary travel. Be watchful as to bonuses. It is *not* money that wins; it is the *merit* of the cause that wins.")

When she died in February, 1973, at the age of ninety-two, she left an estate of $5,250,000.

IX

A produce merchant named George Martin was an old-time friend of Elisabeth Achelis.

One day he came to her and told her that he'd had a dream and that her law firm, Morris and McVeigh, would soon try to declare her incompetent. This, to stop her from spending so much money on her World Calendar cause.

The cause was her child. She called the days of the year "my children."

In a panic, she gave Martin a check for $50,000 with the understanding that he would keep it in trust for the World Calendar.

He kept it for a couple of years. During this time her lawyers made no objection to the money she was

Memo — 13 Sept. 1966

Fee | Expenses
21 July #1000.—
21 Aug 1000.—

15 July #500.—
8 Aug. 500.—
9 " 500.—
10 " 500.—
18 " 500.—
24 . 600.—
1 Sept 600.—
8 " 500.—
7 " 500.—
12 " 500.—
#5200.—

I do not wish to restrict you, but we
cannot afford to be lavish. Travel
expenses are necessary, but plan & reduce, if possible, and guard against
unnecessary travel.
Be watchful as to bonuses.
It is not money that wins;
It is the _merit_ of the cause that wins

Elizabeth

99

spending on her cause. She decided to ask for the return of her $50,000.

Her letters to Martin went unanswered. When she reached him by phone, he was evasive.

At this point she gave me a letter authorizing me to act on her behalf to recover the $50,000.

I went to Martin. I told him she'd take the matter to the Monmouth County prosecutor if he didn't return the money. He was very frightened.

He confessed that he'd given $10,000 to Mrs. Theodora T. Reese as a "commission." He showed me the canceled check, which I photostated. He said she had demanded it because she'd advised Miss Achelis to give him the $50,000.

I insisted that he return $50,000.

He did.

I later discovered that Miss Achelis had paid a gift tax on the $50,000. When she asked for the return of the money, it was because she had been told to do so by Theodora Reese.

X

Theodora Reese was Elisabeth Achelis' closest friend and companion. Miss Achelis had put $250,-000 in trust for her friend Theo. But apparently, Theo wanted some immediate money.

Thus it was that on September 11, 1966, I accepted an invitation to visit Theodora Reese at her modest home in Hopewell Junction, New York.

She told me that she wanted a percentage of the money I got from Miss Achelis. She said she was entitled to it because she was advising Miss Achelis to retain me, and if she told her not to, there would be no more money for me.

"I'll think it over," I said. "You know, I do have expenses, Teddy."

She didn't comment. She was pulling a George Martin on me.

In October, when she didn't hear from me, she visited Miss Achelis's attorney and asked him to draw a Bishop's Report on me.

The report, among other things, showed that I was Jewish.

Elisabeth Achelis was violently anti-Semitic.

On Thursday, November 10, 1966, Guy Rutherfurd, her attorney, called me, and asked me to come to his office. I was given one month's severance pay and told I was fired.

"Why?" I queried.

Rutherfurd said that I had represented myself to Miss Achelis incorrectly in not telling her I was Jewish.

He showed me the Bishop's Report and said that he was sorry but that he could "do nothing."

As I thought about this after I left his office, I became very angry. I went to Richard Wels, who was then my attorney, and he demanded that I be paid for retrieving the $50,000.

The case was finally settled for $2,600. After Wels deducted his fee, I received $1,800.

XI

Now I was without a client. I was a lobbyist with nothing to lobby for. Worse, I had no income.

I continued to see Jerry Ford. I told him that I had lost the World Calendar account.

He seemed genuinely concerned. In retrospect I don't know whether it was for himself or for me.

Nevertheless, until I stopped going to Washington in 1969, I continued to register with the secretary of the Senate and the clerk of the House of Representatives as lobbyist for the calendar reform movement.

Also, until I stopped going to Washington in October, 1969, I continued to "lend" Jerry Ford amounts of money.

XII

In November of 1966, on the shuttle plane back to New York, I discussed my quandary over Ford with Nathan Voloshen.

"I have personal rent and expenses. I have about

$2,000 in savings. But if I keep 'lending' money to
Ford, my money isn't going to hold out very long.
And, frankly, I don't dare stop because I'm afraid of
jeopardizing the relationship. I've set a pattern and
once you do that, it's difficult to break."

Voloshen agreed with me. He cautioned me to
keep in mind that Ford was a very valuable connection.

"If you run short of cash, you can count on me," he
said. Then he added, "But not too often. I'm not a
millionaire."

I did go to him—so often that I probably abused
the privilege.

Once, two years later, when I'd been coming to
him regularly, he remarked half jokingly, "Wait a
minute. You're not my son, you know. Isn't it time
you became self-supporting?" But he continued to
dole out amounts of money.

And Jerry Ford continued to pocket them.

CHAPTER THREE

In January of 1967, Jerry Schiff, a New York accountant I knew, arranged for me to meet with Dr. Albert Buytendorp.

Buytendorp had a problem. His visa had been extended until June 1967. Since it had been extended so frequently—perhaps six or seven times—it could no longer be extended under the U. S. Immigration Law.

He would have to leave the States and return to his native Holland. Then he'd have to wait two years to return to the U.S.A. under the quota for Dutch immigrants. If the Dutch waiting list was larger, he'd have to wait longer.

Buytendorp was an MD. He was a specialist in adolescent psychiatry, a field not generally recognized then in Holland. He worked with several specialists at the Hillside Hospital in Queens. Hillside is a psychiatric hospital. He was nearing forty and two years was a long time. He didn't want to interrupt his work at that stage of his life.

I made an appointment by telephone and then went to Dr. Buytendorp's apartment at 265 West

Eighty-First Street in Manhattan. Schiff, who knew that something "extralegal" had to be done, told me he didn't want to join us. He didn't want to become involved and requested that he not be told anything that happened after the introduction.

After a discussion, Dr. Buytendorp agreed to pay me $1,000 for my services. He said he couldn't afford to pay it all at once. He gave me $250 as a first payment.

We drew up a letter of agreement. In it I promised to use my "best efforts" but added, "I do not claim or guarantee to do anything and/or to fix anything."

The objective was, of course, to keep the doctor in this country despite the law which said he had to leave.

Eventually, I received a total of $2,335 for my services in this matter.

II

Our agreement was dated the 20th of January, 1967.

My first act was to direct Dr. Buytendorp to write a letter to Gerald Ford.

The reason for this was that in case anything came up, there had to be an explanation as to how he got to Ford. We didn't want it known that he was using an "influence peddler" such as myself.

The letter appealed to Ford on the basis of his

being a widely mentioned and powerful member of Congress. It reviewed Buytendorp's history and his problems in getting into the United States. It ended by saying, "Could you please look into the problem which has such serious consequences and which will give such emotional, material, and intellectual hardship at an age and stage in my life when I am ready to produce and give back to society what it has invested in me during the past six years that I have been in the United States."

He gave me the letter. When I offered it to Jerry Ford, I was told to "hang on to it" should it ever be needed.

Then I sent Ford background material and a covering letter. The material included a paper on schizophrenia in an adolescent girl.

It was the beginning of a long and detailed campaign in which Jerry Ford cooperated fully. Without his help and his clout we could have never succeeded.

Incidentally, I made no secret of the fact that I was favoring Representative Ford with money. As the campaign for Dr. Buytendorp stretched out, I explained to the doctor that the money I was asking for expenses included some that had to be paid to Ford for his help.

What follows are a series of fourteen letters that I received from Rep. Gerald Ford with regard to the Buytendorp case.

GERALD R. FORD
FIFTH DISTRICT, MICHIGAN

Congress of the United States
Office of the Minority Leader
House of Representatives
Washington, D.C.

March 7, 1967

Mr. Robert N. Winter-Berger
123 East 75th Street
New York, N. Y. 10021

Dear Bob:

This is just an interim note to let you know that we are getting together all the information we can which might be helpful in Dr. Albert Buytendorp's case.

As indicated to you on the telephone several days ago by one of my staff members, a type of "informal study" has been in the making on the subject of those Mutual Educational and Cultural Exchange Act participants who fall into some category where it might be possible to describe them as being involved in "a program in which the United States Government has an interest." Now, it may develop that there will be no possibility of changing the present approach at all, but I'm interested in it and will let you know soon, I hope.

May I say here that I do know there was some effort by several members of the House and Senate Judiciary Committees several years ago to get something done about certain rigid rules involved with the MECEA administration, and correspondence was exchanged with the State Department in this regard. (As you know, the Judiciary Committees would have jurisdiction over any amendments proposed for this Act.) However, neither Committee has drafted any such proposal.

Warmest personal regards.

Sincerely,

Gerald R. Ford, M. C.

GRF/ed

GERALD R. FORD
FIFTH DISTRICT, MICHIGAN

MICHIGAN OFFICE:
425 CHERRY STREET SE.
GRAND RAPIDS

Congress of the United States
Office of the Minority Leader
House of Representatives
Washington, D.C.

March 22, 1967

Mr. Robert N. Winter-Berger
123 East 75th Street
New York, N.Y. 10021

Dear Bob:

It now appears that the policy and procedure on requests for waivers of the foreign residence requirement of the MECEA will not be changed at this time, although
consideration was given to the whole matter. To complicate matters is all this
talk of our "brain drain" of other countries due to vastly more favorable conditions
for these highly trained professional people.

Therefore, the criteria will remain the same, and Dr. Buytendorp's case will have to
be considered on its individual merits, upon presentation to the HEW Waiver Review
Board of his sponsor's application, substantiated by the strongest possible evidence
to show that Dr. Buytendorp is engaged in a program of high priority to the United
States Government. Also, strong evidence to the effect that Dr. Buytendorp is a
rare asset to this particular nationally significant program, and without whose
continuing contribution to this unique research program, an important part thereof
would have to be discontinued. I think you will agree that this is quite a tall
order.

In the various discussions on this subject we have found it is not possible to determine in advance whether or not any of the programs sponsored by the National Institutes
of Health can be placed in this category. However, I do know that mental health programs are high up on the list of importance. During the processing of any request for
waiver in behalf of anyone working in a program of research sponsored by the National
Institute of Mental Health, of course, the Institute would be asked for its classifi-
cation as to importance nationally, since the Institute sponsors many programs all
over the United States. Thereafter, if it is indicated to the Review Board that the
particular program rates high priority in national interest, the applicant's background
and relationship to the program itself receives the most careful scrutiny and evalu-
ation by the Review Board.

This means that the University applying for the waiver in behalf of Dr. Buytendorp
should very carefully document his background, what he has achieved and has been doing
in the past and is presently doing, what he has published, etc. etc., and should also
submit written statements of various medical authorities, if possible, as to his rare
and important background and stature in his work, which is so vital to the research
program under way.

Mr. Robert Winter-Berger   (re Dr. Buytendorp)

Page 2

I would imagine that the Institute itself would evaluate Dr. Buytendorp's background and importance to the program before the Review Board finally takes up the case for consideration.

As you can readily see, Bob, even if the program is rated as being nationally significant, Dr. Buytendorp must be making a significant contribution to it, and not "just another doctor" working there. This is something that the medical people will have to prove to the satisfaction of the Review Board.

Enclosed are the instructions and forms for the purpose. Although the University must have full knowledge of procedures, perhaps someone in Dr. Buytendorp's behalf should again call attention to the importance of stressing his unique background and vast importance to the program itself.

Incidentally, one of the members of the Review Board happens to be an official at the National Institutes of Health as well. Dr. Buytendorp may know him. He is: Dr. Joe W. Atkinson, Executive Secretary, Surgery B Study Section, Division of Research Grants, Westwood Building - Room 340, National Institutes of Health, Bethesda, Maryland, 20014.

One more thing: any appearance of recruitment by the University must be avoided like poison, since that is considered as the worst possible angle of the problem.

I hope this information will be helpful to you, and I hope it isn't too discouraging. As you readily understand, this is a matter which will hinge entirely on the importance to the United States of the program of research involved and upon the relationship of any particular individual to such a significant program. Of course, this can be evaluated and established only by our medical authorities and the Review Board.

Let me know if there is anything else I can do in the matter. Once all the papers have been sent to the Review Board, if you will let me know, I will then gladly look into the problem further, and see whether it appears any expression of interest on my part to the appropriate authorities would be helpful.

Warmest personal regards and best wishes.

Sincerely,

Gerald R. Ford, M.C.

GRF/ed
Encl.

109

GERALD R. FORD
FIFTH DISTRICT, MICHIGAN

MICHIGAN OFFICE:
425 CHERRY STREET SE.
GRAND RAPIDS

Congress of the United States
Office of the Minority Leader
House of Representatives
Washington, D.C.

June 7, 1967

Mr. Robert N. Winter-Berger
123 East 75th Street
New York, N. Y.   10021

Dear Bob:

This is just a note to let you know I have contacted the Commissioner of Immigration and Naturalization here in Washington concerning the status of Dr. Albert Buytendorp.

I have asked the Commissioner to check the New York City office to insure that Dr. Buytendorp's records are properly marked to indicate the action of the Hillside Hospital in requesting a waiver of the two-year foreign residence requirement of the Mutual Educational and Cultural Exchange Act. This action on the part of Hillside Hospital authorities, of course, covers Dr. Buytendorp's immigration status until the Department of Health, Education and Welfare (Waiver Review Board) has had an opportunity to consider and decide whether the request for waiver can be granted.

Please inform Dr. Buytendorp that he need not have any worry as to the legality of his status, since the action was taken formally before his visa expired on May 25, and automatically keeps him in good standing in every respect under our immigration laws.

Of course, if the waiver request is denied, and Dr. Buytendorp needs some additional time to settle his affairs in this country before returning to the Netherlands, I believe the Immigration Service at New York City will upon his application be able to grant him an extension of 30 days or so for this purpose. However, all of this is considered to be entirely within the law and will not reflect in any way upon Dr. Buytendorp's record.

Sometime later this month I shall be in touch with the officials at the Waiver Review Board to ascertain when a decision can be expected on the waiver request, and will keep you informed as to any developments on Dr. Buytendorp's case.

Warmest personal regards.

Sincerely,

Gerald R. Ford, M. C.

GRF/ed

110

GERALD R. FORD
FIFTH DISTRICT, MICHIGAN

MICHIGAN OFFICE:
425 CHERRY STREET SE.
GRAND RAPIDS

Congress of the United States
Office of the Minority Leader
House of Representatives
Washington, D.C.

September 1, 1967

Mr. Robert N. Winter-Berger
123 East 75th Street
New York, N.Y.   10021

Dear Bob:

It is a pleasure to inform you that I have this morning received word over
the phone concerning approval yesterday by the Waiver Review Board of the
Department of Health, Education and Welfare of the request in behalf of your
friend, Dr. Albert Buytendorp. I expect to obtain formal written confirmation
of this action in about a week or ten days, but had asked that advance information on the decision of the Board at yesterday's meeting be provided, in view
of your concern.

After the Waiver Review Board sends me formal word of its favorable action in
Dr. Buytendorp's case, the file will be sent to the Department of State for a
review of another angle: whether a waiver of the two-year foreign residence
requirement of the Mutual and Cultural Exchange Act in this case would in any
way affect our good relations in MECEA terms with The Netherlands.

As soon as the file is in the hands of the State Department officials handling
such problems, it is my intention to contact the Department to ask that every
consideration, consistent with the pertinent Act, be given to Dr. Buytendorp's
case. I hope your friend will understand that this is a matter over which the
Department has entire jurisdiction and judgment, and the decision will be based
on established criteria in such cases. Generally this procedure takes from two
to three weeks at the Department of State, but I hope to get action expedited
so we can have a decision sooner.

If the Department approves the action of the Waiver Review Board (and I feel sure
it will, barring any special problems) a formal notice will then go from the State
Department to the Immigration authorities in New York. This will open the way for
Dr. Buytendorp to proceed with his application for adjustment of status to that
of a permanent resident, which will be filed in New York, and will then be processed by that office.

I expect to receive advance information from the State Department on their action
before it goes forward to the Immigration authorities in New York, and will let
you know just as soon as I am advised by phone.

Mr. Robert Winter-Berger

Page 2

As you probably know, we have made the big hurdle, and I don't anticipate any
difficulty as far as the confirmation and/or approval of the favorable Waiver
Review Board action is concerned by the State Department.

Thereafter, unless during the investigation of Dr. Buytendorp's background something unfavorable develops, I feel that the Immigration Service processing will
go smoothly.

Warmest personal regards.

Sincerely,

Gerald R. Ford, M. C.

GRF/ed

GERALD R. FORD
FIFTH DISTRICT, MICHIGAN

MICHIGAN OFFICE:
425 CHERRY STREET SE.
GRAND RAPIDS
ZIP 49502

Congress of the United States
Office of the Minority Leader
House of Representatives
Washington, D.C. 20515

September 13, 1967

Mr. Robert N. Winter-Berger
123 East 75th Street
New York, N.Y. 10021

Dear Bob:

Thank you for your letter of the 11th relative to the present status of Dr. Buytendorp's waiver case. I, too, am pleased we've been able to get it into the
right course by obtaining the approval of the Waiver Review Board.

Enclosed is a copy of the letter that reached me in this morning's mail containing formal notice of the Board's action. Also enclosed is a copy of the Board's
letter to Dr. Donald Klein, Director of Research at Hillside Hospital, who will
no doubt be in touch with your friend, Dr. Buytendorp, concerning the status of
the matter as outlined in the letter from Mr. LePine.

The appropriate official at the State Department has been contacted this morning
by telephone concerning my interest in the case, and I hope to have word before
long as to the Department's action. I do not anticipate any difficulty there,
and I shall be in touch with you just as soon as I know what develops.

It is very kind of you to comment so generously about my staff members' work and
attitude, and I appreciate hearing this from you. As you must be aware, Bob, they
all find pleasure in any contacts they have with you in their work. So, the good
feelings are certainly mutual.

Your gracious personal remarks and good wishes are deeply appreciated, I assure
you.

Warmest personal regards.

Sincerely

Gerald R. Ford, M. C.

GRF/ed
Encl.

GERALD R. FORD
FIFTH DISTRICT, MICHIGAN

MICHIGAN OFFICE:
425 CHERRY STREET SE.
GRAND RAPIDS

Congress of the United States
Office of the Minority Leader
House of Representatives
Washington, D.C. 20515

October 11, 1967

Mr. Robert N. Winter-Berger
123 East 75th Street
New York, N.Y. 10021

Dear Bob:

We were advised on October 6 in a telephone message from the Department of State that approval of waiver for Dr. Albert Buytendorp was being recommended by the Department in a letter to the Immigration and Naturalization Service in New York City.

However, it is my understanding that it may take several weeks before Dr. Buytendorp is advised of this action by the Immigration authorities, due to the time required for processing, etc. At that time, if the Immigration authorities concur, Dr. Buytendorp will be informed of the next step he may take -- application for adjustment of status to that of a permanent resident.

So that you will have an idea of what follows, I am sending you sample forms of the kind Dr. Buytendorp will no doubt receive from the Immigration and Naturalization Service in New York City for completion and filing.

As soon as Dr. Buytendorp presents the completed forms to the Immigration and Naturalization Service, processing of his case will commence through the channels of the Service here and abroad, wherever Dr. Buytendorp has lived over a period of six months since he reached age 16. This processing and background investigation is what would be undertaken by American Consular authorities in the Netherlands if Dr. Buytendorp had applied for an immigrant visa instead of the Exchange Act (temporary) visa he applied for before he entered the United States. However, for the immigrant type visa application the background investigation is far more careful and complete, and for this reason takes many months to complete.

In all probability there will be no obstacles in Dr. Buytendrop's background, and it will simply be a question of time before a visa can be approved for him.

Should Dr. Buytendorp not receive any word from the Immigration Service by the first week in November, if you care to have me do so I will gladly contact the Commissioner's office here to find out what is holding matters up.

Warmest personal regards.

Sincerely,

Gerald R. Ford, M. C.
GRF/ed/encl.

GERALD R. FORD
FIFTH DISTRICT, MICHIGAN

MICHIGAN OFFICE:
425 CHERRY STREET SE.
GRAND RAPIDS
ZIP 49502

Congress of the United States
Office of the Minority Leader
House of Representatives
Washington, D.C. 20515

November 28, 1967

Mr. Robert N. Winter-Berger
123 East 75th Street
New York, N.Y. 10021

Dear Bob:

The forms I ordered from the Commissioner of Immigration and Naturalization here
in Washington and from the Visa Office of the Department of State have all been
finally received at my office for Dr. Buytendorp's case, and I am enclosing these
for his use.

Under recent changes in the Immigration and Nationality Act, those persons born in
Western Hemisphere countries cannot adjust status without leaving the United States
temporarily in order to complete the requirements for an immigrant visa in one of
our Consulates abroad. In earlier years Canada and Mexico cooperated by allowing
aliens residing in the United States on visitor or student visas and who were in the
process of adjusting their status to enter their countries on a temporary basis in
order to complete processing of their applications for visas. This is no longer
possible since the Canadian and Mexican Governments now admit such aliens only if
a written guarantee from United States authorities that they will be re-admitted
to this country is submitted before admission to those countries. Under the circum-
stance that United States authorities cannot make such guarantees before one of its
Consuls abroad determines whether such applicants are admissible under our laws, it
is therefore necessary that applications be made elsewhere.

May I add here that the only exceptions (as far as admitting U.S. resident aliens
to Canada or Mexico for the purpose of awaiting final determination on adjustment
of their status to permanent residency here) would be: 1. When the alien involved
is the spouse, child or parent of a U.S. citizen, and 2. When the alien cannot return to his home country because of fear of persecution on account of race, religion
or political beliefs.

In order to assist Dr. Buytendorp as much as possible in completing all necessary
formalities and processsing of his case before he actually returns to the Netherlands,
please ask him to complete the enclosed forms in accordance with the attached instructions, and mail them to: American Consul General, American Consulate General, Vlasmarkt 1, Rotterdam, Netherlands.

If you will let me know when Dr. Buytendorp has mailed the forms to Rotterdam, I will
gladly follow through by sending a letter to the American Consul General to ask that
the quickest possible processing and background investigation be given to Dr. Buytendorp's case.

Mr. Robert N. Winter-Berger

Page 2

Whether this preliminary processing can be completed in two or three weeks or in two or three months depends upon how quickly the information can be obtained by those charged with the responsibility of handling the processing and investigation of such cases. However, please advise Dr. Buytendorp that I very much doubt this can be accomplished in time for him to return home for Christmas. The reply I hope to receive from the Consul General after Dr. Buytendorp has sent in all of his papers will be a guide for him in this respect.

In the meantime, if Dr. Buytendorp's passport must be renewed by the Netherlands Consul in New York City or in Washington, I would suggest that he do this in plenty of time. He no doubt has done this on earlier occasions with the Netherlands Consul and is familiar with the procedure.

In this connection (since the I-94 form mentioned in the Justice Department's letter to him of November 16 is attached to his passport) please make sure that Dr. Buytendorp first complies with the request of Mr. Esperdy that he bring in his passport before December 15 so that his status can be verified. At that time he should, of course, inform the Immigration Service that he is taking appropriate steps with the American Consul General at Rotterdam to obtain an immigrant visa. If he is still in the process of completing the forms at the time he goes to the Immigration Service, he should by all means indicate this, and that it is his intention to travel to Rotterdam just as soon as the Consul General informs him that preliminary processing of his application for immigrant visa has been completed.

I believe the Immigration Service is fully aware that the processing of Dr. Buytendorp's application for immigrant visa may very well take up to several months, and will mark his records accordingly. This will cover him until he is ready to leave for Rotterdam.

I hope all will go well and that you will let me know how matters are proceeding so that I can be helpful at the proper time.

It was good to see you last week.

Warmest personal regards.

Sincerely,

Gerald R. Ford, M. C.

GRF/ed/encl.

Mr. Robert N. Winter-Berger

Page 3

P.S. The forms enclosed are: a. Preliminary Questionnaire To Determine Immigrant
Status (Form 497) -- 1 copy to be sent to Consul
General. (Information sheet 852 also enclosed.)
   b. Application For Alien Employment Certification --
Part A (Form ES-575A) -- 2 copies to be sent to
Consul General. (Instructions also enclosed.)
   c. Biographic Data For Visa Purposes (Form DSP70) --
1 copy for each place Dr. Buytendorp resided since
reaching age 14 -- to be sent to Consul General.

Of the foregoing I have provided an additional copy of each so a record of what goes
forward to the Consul General is readily available in the United States should the
need arise at some time during the processing of Dr. Buytendorp's visa application.

Please be sure to have Dr. Buytendorp send the original letter he received from the
Immigration and Naturalization Service concerning the approval of his waiver. Without
that letter the Consul General will not be able to even commence the processing of
his application.

GRF

THE GERALD FORD LETTERS

GERALD R. FORD
FIFTH DISTRICT, MICHIGAN

MICHIGAN OFFICE:
425 CHERRY STREET SE.
GRAND RAPIDS
ZIP 49502

Congress of the United States
Office of the Minority Leader
House of Representatives
Washington, D.C. 20515

January 18, 1968

Mr. Robert N. Winter-Berger
123 East 75th Street
New York, N.Y. 10021

Dear Bob:

Enclosed are the additional forms you requested when you were at my office yesterday.

Please have Dr. Buytendorp get going on completion and mailing of these immediately since time is now of the essence.

However, there appears to be the need to file a preference petition with the Immigration Service in New York, in addition to the forms you already know about. This due to the fact that we are coming up to a great change in rules and regulations on visa applicants because of the operation of the amendments to the Immigration and Nationality Act in December of 1965. The new rules will go into effect in June. Since the quota to which Dr. Buytendorp is chargeable (Surinam, because of his birth there) may very well become oversubscribed very shortly, it is most important that he get his preference petition in -- for third preference under the quota. The date of __approval__ of that third preference petition will be Dr. Buytendorp's __priority date__ under the quota. So the sooner he gets the petition filed with the Immigration Service, the quicker he will get on the approved list, which is kept in the chronological order of approval.

Accordingly, as soon as he has completed the forms for the Consulate General in Rotterdam, they should be mailed. Immediately thereafter he should have the Hospital complete the enclosed Petition to Classify Preference Status of Alien in his behalf and have it filed. Among other supporting documents for this Petition you will see under item 6 of the instructions attached thereto that a form ES 575A is required for this action also. So, I am enclosing two additional copies of that form for his convenience. Perhaps he should check the list of documents required for this petition for it may be that some of these are the same as those required for the Consulate General at Rotterdam. In this connection I call your attention to item 7 regarding the rules for documents. You will see that he can take with him to the Immigration Service photostats of the originals also required by Consular authorities, and have the receiving officer check on the photostats that they are exact copies of the originals which he is required to send on to Rotterdam, immediately returning the originals to him. In this way he will not need to obtain additional original documents and hold up the processing for some time.

If you have any questions please don't hesitate to call Mrs. Dukov in my office.

My very best to you.

Sincerely,

Gerald R. Ford, M. C.
GRF/ed/encl.

GERALD R. FORD
FIFTH DISTRICT, MICHIGAN

MICHIGAN OFFICE:
425 CHERRY STREET SE.
GRAND RAPIDS
ZIP 49502

Congress of the United States
Office of the Minority Leader
House of Representatives
Washington, D.C. 20515

February 19, 1968

Mr. Robert N. Winter-Berger
123 East 75th Street
New York, N.Y. 10021

Dear Bob:

Just a note to tell you I am writing to the American Consul General in Rotterdam relative to my interest in the case of Dr. Buytendorp. I am asking that processing of his papers be expedited as much as possible to the point where Dr. Buytendorp can make plans for a visit to the Netherlands and his formal appearance before Consular officials can be made preparatory to visa issuance, which is required by our immigration laws.

I hope to have a report from the Consul General or one of his Consuls there as to the approximate time Dr. Buytendorp may be required to wait before he may proceed to Rotterdam, and also as to the need for anything additional in the way of papers. There isn't anything I can think of which would be required since all the important facts have been amply covered I believe by the papers already submitted to the Rotterdam Consular office.

The worst is over, Bob, I think, and it is now a question of how much time it will take for our authorities to accomplish the investigation, etc. in the Netherlands and here in the United States wherever Dr. Buytendorp has lived.

My very best to you.

Sincerely,

Gerald R. Ford, M. C.

GRF/ed

GERALD R. FORD
FIFTH DISTRICT, MICHIGAN

MICHIGAN OFFICE:
425 CHERRY STREET SE.
GRAND RAPIDS
ZIP 49502

Congress of the United States
Office of the Minority Leader
House of Representatives
Washington, D.C. 20515

April 9, 1968

Mr. Robert Winter-Berger
123 East 75th Street
New York, N.Y. 10021

Dear Bob:

Enclosed are the two statements you sent down from Dr. Buytendorp and which will be needed for his file in Rotterdam as indicated by the instructions he received from the Consul General.

In taking this case up with the Visa Office we were given to understand that there will be no change in the rule that he as an applicant for adjustment of status born in the Western Hemisphere will be required to apply for a visa at one of our Consulates abroad. The recent documentary requirements were made in an effort to insure that he can be charged to the Dutch quota instead of the Surinam quota because there is greater likelihood that numbers in the third preference portion will be available under the Dutch quota.

I am today sending a letter to our Consul General in Rotterdam, again calling his attention to my interest in Dr. Buytendorp's case, and advising him that all the documents he requested have been obtained, and that Dr. Buytendorp will be in touch with him in the next day or so. Of course, I will ask that the case be processed as quickly as possible, and that Dr. Buytendorp be alerted in advance as to the date he should appear in person at the Consulate General for final visa formalities.

Let's hope it won't take too long after all Dr. Buytendorp's papers have been submitted to conduct the necessary investigation, etc.

In any case, don't hesitate to contact us here if we need to lend a hand.

I'll let you know what I learn from the Consul General just as soon as information is received here.

Warmest personal regards.

Gerald R. Ford, M. C.

GRF/ed
Encl.

P.S. Please drop me a note if the Immigration Service in New York does not inform Dr. Buytendorp sometime next week of preference approval. Also let me know when Dr. Buytendorp has followed through with the Consul General on the question of the documents requested.

GERALD R. FORD
FIFTH DISTRICT, MICHIGAN

MICHIGAN OFFICE:
425 CHERRY STREET SE.
GRAND RAPIDS
ZIP 49502

Congress of the United States
Office of the Minority Leader
House of Representatives
Washington, D.C. 20515

April 16, 1968

Mr. Robert N. Winter-Berger
123 East 75th Street
New York, N.Y. 10021

Dear Bob:

Just a note to let you know that the Commissioner of Immigration has today obtained information (in response to my request) to the effect that the petition of the Hillside Hospital to grant Dr. Buytendorp third preference under the quota has been approved.

Accordingly, the Consul General at Rotterdam will be informed of this action and Dr. Buytendorp's file will be marked to show this.

Hillside Hospital will be informed also, but it may be a week or so before the information sifts down to that office and Dr. Buytendorp. So I thought I would give you and the good doctor this bit of news -- to alleviate some of his worry.

Now all we need to work on is the processing by the Consul General. As I indicated to you in my recent letter, I again wrote to the Consul General about the case. No reply has come in yet.

I must say that this has indeed been an unusual case in that there appeared to be so many stumbling blocks at every step, despite the fact that we were able to get the most important step of the waiver accomplished without too much delay. Well, let's hope Dr. Buytendorp will have smooth sailing in his case from here on in.

My best to you, Bob.

Sincerely,

Gerald R. Ford, M. C.

GRF/ed

GERALD R. FORD
FIFTH DISTRICT, MICHIGAN

MICHIGAN OFFICE:
425 CHERRY STREET SE.
GRAND RAPIDS
ZIP 49502

Congress of the United States
Office of the Minority Leader
House of Representatives
Washington, D.C. 20515

April 19, 1968

Mr. Robert N. Winter-Berger
123 East 75th Street
New York, N.Y.   10021

Dear Bob:

I have your letter of the 15th, indicating that you have succeeded in having
Dr. Buytendorp round up all necessary papers for the Consul General, and enclosing a copy of the your letter to the Consul General.

Enclosed is a copy of the letter that reached me this afternoon from the Consul
General in reply to my letter of April 9 in behalf of Dr. Buytendorp. As you
will see, he states that he did not receive the letter I sent to him earlier
concerning my interest in the case. In my letter of April 9 to the Consul General
I had enclosed a copy of that February 17 letter -- since I could not understand
why no reply had been forthcoming from him.

In the meantime, I am sure he will receive Dr. Buytendorp's letter of April 15
by today or tomorrow at the latest. I feel certain also that the processing will
be handled in an expeditious manner, especially in view of the fact that Dr. Buytendorp has been able to assemble all the documentation to allow chargeability
under the Dutch quota.

So, now you may tell Dr. Buytendorp to be patient a little while longer, so that
the investigative process can be completed in each place he resided over six
months after he reached age 16.

The minute we hear anything here in Washington about developments, you will be
alerted accordingly.

Warmest personal regards.

Sincerely,

Gerald R. Ford, M. C.

GRF/ed
Encl.

THE GERALD FORD LETTERS

GERALD R. FORD
FIFTH DISTRICT, MICHIGAN

MICHIGAN OFFICE:
425 CHERRY STREET SE.
GRAND RAPIDS
ZIP 49502

Congress of the United States
Office of the Minority Leader
House of Representatives
Washington, D.C. 20515

April 26, 1968

Mr. Robert N. Winter-Berger
123 East 75th Street
New York, N.Y. 10021

Dear Bob:

You will be pleased to see the enclosed copy of the notification which just
reached me from our Consul General in Rotterdam, indicating that an appointment
has been set up for Dr. Buytendorp to appear with his papers at the Consulate
on May 13.

Generally, if the applicant for a visa is found to be eligible in every respect
for a visa on the appointment date for his formal application, and passes the
routine physical examination, his visa is issued that very same day or within
a day or so thereafter. So, we have every reason to feel that the case will
be closed out on May 13.

In all probability a notice to appear has been sent to Dr. Buytendorp, but I
wanted you to have this copy for your own records.

If for any reason Dr. Buytendorp cannot make arrangements to be in Rotterdam
on May 13, please ask him to immediately write to the Honorable Seaborn P. Foster,
American Consul General, Vlasmarkt 1, Rotterdam, explaining that he cannot leave
his work on time to make that date, and ask for a date within a week or two after
that. I feel sure the Consul General would make appropriate arrangements to ac-
commodate Dr. Buytendorp.

However, ask Dr. Buytendorp not to postpone matters if he can possibly avoid
doing so, since the quota situation is really getting bad in all of our Consulates.

Please keep us advised down here as to developments, so we can give a hand if that
is necessary.

Warmest personal regards.

Sincerely,

Gerald R. Ford, M. C.
GRF/ed/encl.

123

GERALD R. FORD
FIFTH DISTRICT, MICHIGAN

MICHIGAN OFFICE:
425 CHERRY STREET SE.
GRAND RAPIDS
ZIP 49502

Congress of the United States
Office of the Minority Leader
House of Representatives
Washington, D.C. 20515

May 20, 1968

Mr. Robert N. Winter-Berger
123 East 75th Street
New York, N.Y.   10021

Dear Bob:

I hasten to send you the enclosed copy of the notification that arrived this morning from the Consulate General in Rotterdam, containing information that a visa was issued to Dr. Butendorp on May 14.

You will be relieved, I know, and I am delighted that all went well after the Consul General had his personal attention called to the case.

It has been a pleasure for me to get this worked out for you. It's really been like a game of chess, hasn't it?

Warmest personal regards.

Sincerely,

Gerald R. Ford, M.C.

GRF/ed
encl.

CHAPTER FOUR

I have, in my time, lied. I'm a human being with all the weaknesses and frailties of human beings.

Some of my lies were real lies and some were what people at times refer to as "white lies."

The "white lie" is one intended to avoid hurting someone. At the same time it is supposedly "harmless."

I told a "white lie" in *The Washington Pay-Off*, and it has come back to haunt me.

It was told with good intentions.

When I wrote and dictated the material that filled the pages of *The Washington Pay-Off*, I was very ambivalent about Jerry Ford. I'd been closer to him than to anyone else in Washington.

Although I knew that I would be attacked and ostracized for daring to reveal what I'd done and what I knew, I believed that I was performing an important public service.

Foolishly, at the same time I wanted Jerry Ford to know that he was one person against whom I didn't feel hostility. I tried to get the message to him by writing: "Ford was the only politician I met in

Washington who, to the best of my knowledge, would not accept a campaign contribution in cash. He always insisted on a check, and he always specified how he wanted the check to be made out."

(Yet, without explaining to the reader what I really meant, I noted on page 245 that, "I already had a lot riding on Gerald Ford." This referred to the period before I made my first campaign contribution by check.)

In my own mind I rationalized that I was talking about "campaign contributions" and my "loans" to him couldn't be considered that. Too, I felt that I was protecting myself. I didn't want the Internal Revenue Service challenging my "expense" deductions. Nor did I want to include anything in the book that couldn't in some way be supported by documents.

My "loans" had been in cash. No receipts. No witnesses.

As I noted earlier, I wasn't sure of the legality of any of the money I was "lending" to Jerry Ford.

Later in the book I said: "Unlike Speaker McCormack, who was always ready and willing to accept a campaign contribution in cash, Jerry Ford always insisted on checks. I never knew him to accept cash from anybody. And once the money issue was settled, Jerry Ford probably worked harder to carry out his end of the bargain—that is, to pay a favor for value received—than anybody else I knew in Washington."

That was twice.

I thought Jerry Ford would appreciate and understand that I was expressing "good feelings" and friendship for him in an "inside" way.

II

When *The Washington Pay-Off* was published, Lyle Stuart received a phone call from Washington. Robert Lewis of the Booth Newspapers and Richard Ryan of the Detroit *News* had questioned Ford about the statements in my book.

Ford said he scarcely knew me and hadn't written more than five or six letters to me.

Stuart asked the newsmen to stand by. He put them on "hold" and phoned me at home.

"Bob," he said, "I have two newspaper reporters on another line who say Ford insists he scarcely knew you. He told them that he didn't write more than six letters to you."

"But we have close to fifty of his letters in the safe deposit box!" I exclaimed.

"I know, Bob. The question is are you willing to show them if these fellows make a special trip to New York?"

"It's okay with me if it's okay with you."

Stuart made his offer. The two men accepted and on the following Monday, April 17, 1972, Lewis and Ryan met me at the Manufacturers Hanover Trust Company branch at Eleventh Street and Broadway in lower Manhattan. There I let them examine a large portion of the mail I'd received from Ford.

They spent the day with me. I wined them and dined them for lunch. At one point, Lewis asked me point-blank if Ford had ever asked for or received cash.

I realized that they were investigating charges in the book and that I should be consistent. I recall feeling somewhat uncomfortable for they both stared at me when I replied, "I don't recall Jerry Ford ever personally receiving a cent from me."

Now I had told the "white lie" three times.

III

Both men appeared to be impressed with the material. I was annoyed that Jerry had made such a foolish statement, especially after I'd gone out of my way to shield him. The newsmen assured me that they were going to write true and exciting stories. The story should make front page headlines, they said, what with Ford saying he'd written only five or six letters and my collection of nearly fifty.

There were no "headline stories." There were no wire service stories. All I ever saw was one rather biased article by Lewis. It was slanted to favor Ford. It never mentioned the fact that Lewis and Ryan had seen far more than the five or six letters Ford said he wrote to me.

Recently I couldn't help but wonder whether they
might have been sent by Ford to look at what I had
and to see if I would stick to the story that I'd never
given him any cash.

IV

I was going to "Daddy" Voloshen and being a
courier for the cash payments to Ford. Obviously,
Voloshen thought he too could make excellent use of
my close ties with Jerry Ford, should a profitable
opportunity arise.

On January 27, 1970, a column by Jack Anderson
began by saying:

> The respected name of House GOP Leader Ger-
> ald Ford has been caught up in the investigation of
> fixer Nathan Voloshen and House aide Martin
> Sweig.
> The two wheeler-dealers have been indicted by a
> New York Grand Jury for using House Speaker
> John McCormack's office for influence peddling.
> This column has now learned that a third member
> of their fixit team, Robert Winter-Berger, operated
> occasionally out of Ford's office.
> Winter-Berger has avoided prosecution by coop-
> erating with the Grand Jury. He is expected to
> appear as a government witness against Voloshen
> and Sweig at their trial.

The column went on to say that Assistant Attorney General Will Wilson "who runs the Justice Department's Criminal Division, paid a secret call upon Ford to question him about Winter-Berger ... Ford recalled that Winter-Berger had come to his office 'well recommended,' but couldn't recall who had recommended him."

V

Voloshen wasn't angry with me. He was an old pro and completely understood my position. He knew that I was trying to save my own skin.

Right after the Anderson column appeared, we got together.

I told him that I'd decided not to visit Ford's office again. Previously I had mentioned that I was avoiding Ford until the investigation was over.

Voloshen seemed to have assumed that when things calmed down, he could use me by having me ask Ford to help him.

But now, after he reread Jack Anderson's column, he remarked wryly, "Well, Bob, there goes about fourteen thousand American dollars down the drain."

I did some quick mental arithmetic. Most of the money I had given to Ford came from Voloshen. In addition, there was the earlier money and at least a few other "out of pocket gifts" of my own. In all, I estimated I had "loaned" Gerald Ford about $15,000.

VI

In *The Washington Pay-Off* I had said:

> As a result of the Voloshen-Sweig indictments, other criminal investigations were started. In the deal for the light sentence Voloshen received was his agreement to cooperate in any other investigations which might develop.
>
> One such [investigation] was conducted by the New York State Joint Legislative Committee on Crime [chaired by the late John H. Hughes], before whom I was called to testify three times in 1970. Since I was confident that the Eddie Gilbert case would come up, I insisted on having Richard Wels present each time as my attorney. I wanted him there so he could hear for himself anything I might say about the case that could involve him. . . . As it turned out, however, I was not questioned very thoroughly along these lines.

I tried to avoid contributing new material against Voloshen by indicating that in the period before May, 1967, I had seen him only a few times and those usually by accident.

A sampling of the letters of summons I received from him obviously contradict this. It is obvious that if I skipped seeing him for a week or two, he became annoyed. Included also is a bill made out to Voloshen in 1965 with his own handwritten instructions on how to prepare it.

From the desk of

Nathan Voloshen

Dear Bob -

It is important that y- get in touch with me immediately -

I want no delay as this is important to you at once

Nat V.

NATHAN VOLOSHEN
6 EAST 45ᵀᴴ STREET
NEW YORK 17, N. Y.

August 31, 1965.

Bob, please call me upon receipt of this note.

Nat Voloshen.

Dec. 10/1965

$
3500

for year 1965

For Professor Lewis

Undated + Nuclear Wills

December 10th, 1965

Mr. Nathan Voloshen
6 East 45th Street
New York, N.Y. 10017

For public relations services rendered
for year 1965   -------- $3,500.00

PAID

NATHAN VOLOSHEN
6 EAST 45ᵀᴴ STREET
NEW YORK 17, N.Y.

December 14,1965.

Mr. Winterberger, Mr. Voloshen said please
call him without fail. He will be in the
office on Thursday.

                    Margaret.

NATHAN VOLOSHEN
6 EAST 45ᵀᴴ STREET
NEW YORK 17, N.Y.

March 8, 1966.

Dear Bob,

      I am losing patience with your
many promises. I want to see you Thursday
without fail. Don't let me write you
again.

      Nat.

NATHAN VOLOSHEN
6 EAST 45ᵀᴴ STREET
NEW YORK 17, N. Y.

April 23,1966.

Dear Mr. Winterberg:

Mr. V asked me to drop
you a line and tell you he would like to hear
from you Wednesday morning, April 27th,
with fail.

Cordially,

Margaret
Margaret

CHAPTER FIVE

John Nance Garner remarked to Lyndon Johnson in 1960, "I'll tell you Lyndon, the vice-presidency isn't worth a pitcher of warm spit."

Nevertheless, when the news came that Richard Nixon had selected Jerry Ford to succeed Spiro Agnew, I was quite disturbed. It meant that Ford would succeed Nixon on the event of death, impeachment, serious illness, etc.

This was before Anthony Lewis would write in the *New York Times*, "It is really a mystery that any conservatives should still regard Richard Nixon as one of their own. He is something very different: a man without roots, without respect for tradition, without consciousness of moral responsibility, without feeling for institutions except the desire to use them. His tax behavior is a fair example.

"Trying to deduct the cost of a masked ball [for his daughter] as 'expenses incurred in the performance of official functions as President of the United States' is not our national standard of tax ethics."

I had known for some time that Nixon was a bad egg. Every lobbyist I knew shared my feelings that

139

under Nixon and his crew (whom Stewart Alsop was to call "the vipers' nest in the White House") practically everything in the government was for sale at a price.

It was good hunting weather for lobbyists but not a good time for the country.

I suddenly felt that I owed my country what it would cost me to tell about the $15,000.

Edmund Burke had long ago noted that "All that is necessary for evil to triumph is for good men to do nothing."

I didn't believe that Jerry Ford was the devil incarnate, but I did know that he was less than the "honest Jerry Ford" image that was already being projected by the profile painters.

II

I'm not an uncommonly brave man, and I knew that once I opened my mouth, I would be touching a tender nerve among the people who manage America. I would bring the wrath of the establishment down upon me.

I knew this and yet still felt, naively perhaps, that if the truth were told, people would understand that Jerry was a nice guy but not someone you'd want to trust to perform open heart surgery on you.

And it was becoming more and more evident each day that America needed some open heart surgery.

Never before had so few Americans believed in their rulers. Never before had faith in our institutions and our way of life been at such a low ebb.

A still small voice told me, "Bob, forget it. You'll only make trouble for yourself."

How could I prove anything? I had no records. No check stubs. No witnesses. I was a little man of no large consequence, and I would be facing the Congress of the United States, one of the closest knit fraternities in the world.

I decided, nevertheless, to tell the truth and take the consequences.

III

Like the boy who cried "wolf" until nobody believed him when a wolf really attacked his flock, I was now in the position of having said three times that Ford never took cash.

But he did. $15,000 worth of it—more or less.

I state this on my life and on my mother's life.

And I repeat what I told the Senate Committee on Rules and Administration: I will take a lie-detector test at any place and at any time.

And if Gerald Ford is innocent—as he claims—I strongly urge him to do likewise.

The American people deserve to have all doubt removed as to which of us is lying.

I said earlier and I say now that Gerald Ford is a

nice, easygoing fellow. But he is as corrupt and as much "for sale" as any other grafting politician.

And the American people deserved better than having a President Ford in their future.

CHAPTER SIX

I am not a sympathizer or admirer of the late Whittaker Chambers, but I think I know how he must have felt during the early days of his hearings when nobody believed him.

I was to feel that way.

I had anticipated that the congressional establishment would try to challenge my information, but I didn't foresee how thoroughly they would try to hold me up to ridicule and try to destroy any chance of the public believing one word of what I had to say.

I was a goat among the gladiators.

It took me a while to realize it.

The drama began on Wednesday, October 24. A publisher named Thomas Lipscomb called me. He had given me the first $10,000 of a $20,000 advance against royalties to write a book about corruption in California and Texas. His publishing house of Mason & Lipscomb seemed to have unlimited money and very effective pipelines everywhere from the Senate to the CIA.

Lipscomb told me that he'd visited Jack Anderson's office and had arranged an appointment for me to tell my story there.

When I arrived, Anderson wasn't around. His assistant, Les Whitten, was.

In retrospect, I cannot help but feel that I walked into a setup. For example, I had no way of knowing that Anderson was about to take the line that whatever Gerald Ford's limitations were, he was an "honest man." Muckraker Anderson had become part of the Greek chorus who seemed to think they had to save the Republic by convincing the mob that the clay figure in front of them was really made of precious marble.

I told Whitten the story of my cash payments to Gerald Ford.

He listened and then asked if I would sign an affidavit that he would dictate.

"This is just to cover us on anything we might decide to use in the column," he assured me.

I said yes.

Whitten dictated a rough résumé of what I'd said. Jack Anderson's secretary took the dictation. After each paragraph, Whitten turned to me and asked, "Is that right?"

When he said, "The money came from my personal income, and I paid taxes on it," I nodded dumbly. I hadn't paid taxes on it. It was only in part—perhaps 10 or 15 percent—my own money. The large part of it was, of course, Nathan Voloshen's money. That plus the contributions from Elisabeth Achelis.

The pressure of the moment kept me from correcting him. He had been urging me to hurry; the column had to go over the wires that very day. And

144

Lipscomb, who was present and seemed intent on scoring a "coup" with the article, also pressed me to sign. I suppose it was sheer stupidity not to have my lawyer present, but I was in the spotlight again, a sudden "star" in the big colosseum.

Nevertheless the matter bothered me. A few days later I notified Whitten of the error in his affidavit. (This was quite some time before my appearance before the Senate committee.)

I explained that, in the excitement, I hadn't had time to think it through, and the fact was that I hadn't paid tax on most of the money given to Ford because I was only a conduit for the cash.

Whitten apologized for not having given me time to read over and consider the affidavit. He said that the reason there had been such a rush was that the column was to go out that very day. He assured me that there was nothing to worry about.

I was gullible enough to believe him.

What actually happened was this: one hour after I signed the "hurry up" affidavit, Richard Casad made his appearance. Whitten identified him as an investigator for the Senate Rules Committee, which had the Gerald Ford vice-presidential nomination under consideration. I was told that Casad was on special loan to the committee by Senator Jackson.

In the course of our conversation, Casad asked me if he could have a copy of the affidavit.

Whitten said he could have the original provided that he would keep it in his possession until Monday, October 29th. Whitten wanted to have the exclusive story about the $15,000 that was "loaned" to Ford, and he didn't want anyone on the committee to leak the store before the Anderson column appeared. Casad agreed.

On October 25th, I spent four hours with Casad. At that time I told him of the mistake in the Whitten affidavit. He told me it didn't matter since a second affidavit would be drawn up for the Senate Rules Committee, based on his own investigation. On October 26th I spent another five hours with him. The nine hours were used to go over all my documents in my New York bank vault.

Casad also asked if I'd appear voluntarily before the committee on November 7th. I agreed.

On two occasions, in the ensuing days, Casad phoned me to say he had been too busy to prepare the affidavit and to excuse the delay but that it would be coming any day.

Finally, on November 3, a Saturday, I called Casad's Washington, D. C. office at 12:30 P.M. The girl who answered didn't know if he'd be back that day. I asked about the affidavit. She said she didn't know anything about it.

At 2:30, Casad contacted me. He told me that I was no longer a voluntary witness.

Surprised, I asked him why the change.

He said that the committee had voted in executive session on the previous afternoon that I was to be subpoenaed and that there was to be no affidavit submitted to me.

I asked him the difference between being a voluntary witness and being subpoenaed.

His exact words to me, which I noted on a pad of paper, were, "You're going to be massaged by the committee.

II

I was scared.

Friends warned me that the committee would destroy me. They would jail me. They would entrap me. I had challenged the sanctity of Congress. They were not going to let me get away with it.

Looking at the players was not reassuring.

In *The Washington Pay-Off* I had described how I got Senator Claiborne Pell out of jail after he'd been arrested for being in a raided gay bar in Greenwich Village.

The evening before my appearance, I visited Lyle Stuart at his apartment.

"Stop being afraid," he said. "Just tell the truth."

I told him about the frightening warnings of friends.

"First of all," Stuart said, "you don't have to be afraid of them. They're afraid of you. They don't know what you'll come up with. Keep that in mind: they're afraid of you."

Stuart became thoughtful. "Do you know what I'd do if I were you? I'd demand a public hearing. I'd first ask to tape the proceedings myself. They'll

147

probably tell you you can't. Then I'd demand either a public hearing or that the press be allowed to be present. In view of what's happening in this country what with wiretapping, erased tapes, our devious president, the thieving vice-president ... and in view of what happens with the judiciary too, I would take the valid position that the press is the last bastion of democracy. If it weren't for the press, Agnew would still be receiving his cash bribes and Nixon would be enriching himself many millions of dollars more. Tell them either you want the press present or a public hearing. Or tell them to fuck off."

I left Stuart's apartment in better spirits.

Unfortunately, I didn't follow his advice.

Ironically, less than three weeks later, Chester Davis, who runs the Howard Hughes casinos and is a key man in the Hughes organization, took just that position with the Ervin committee. He said he would testify but only in public hearings.

III

First the committee heard Dr. Hutschnecker.

He denied that Ford had ever been his patient. He admitted that he'd met with him once for fifteen minutes when I'd introduced the two men.

As I pointed out conclusively in my Les Whitten affidavit, it was not "fifteen minutes" but one hour and fifteen minutes. I had time to go to my apartment, which was around the corner, and make my lunch. And when I returned an hour later, the two men were still together.

I recalled that one day Hutschnecker had told me, "You know I spent an hour and a half with Jerry this past Saturday when I was in Washington."

I was surprised. "I didn't know you were seeing him at all."

"Oh, yes," he said, "we've been in contact since you introduced us."

I thought it would be tactless to question Hutschnecker further for I assumed that he meant that Jerry had been seeing him for psychotherapy.

The next time I saw Ford, a day or two later, I said to him, "I understand you saw Hutschie for an hour and a half last Saturday."

"Yes, I had an interesting conversation with him," he replied. Then he clammed up.

I again assumed that the two men had been seeing each other professionally. After all, an hour and a half was a long time out of the busy schedule of the minority leader of the House of Representatives.

IV

On November 16, 1973, Jack Anderson reported:

Vice-President-designate Gerald Ford dished money out of his own campaign funds for two members of Congress who sit on the committees now investigating him [Senator Griffin and Congressman Lott].

Two separate $1,000 transfers were made from Ford's fund to political committees supporting the re-election of Sen. Griffin (R-Mich) on October 24th, 1972, and November 1st, 1972. Griffin is a member of the Senate Rules Committee which has been conducting hearings on the Ford nomination.

Griffin conceded that he hadn't told Rules Committee chairman Cannon (D-Nev) about the $2,000 turnover but contended, "This is no more a conflict of interest than the fact that Ford has been a close friend of mine for 25 years."

V

The witness was Alice Weston, the woman who introduced me to Ford and to whom I paid $1,000 for the introduction.

Her testimony was that she had never received any money from me.

The more intensely she protested, the more obvious it became to me that the two $500 cash payments I made to her were not reported on her income tax returns. But in order to make her point, she testified under oath that "We had no discussion about money. He did not pay me one penny. And I paid my own way to Washington and back."

Chairman Howard W. Cannon then asked, "Did he reimburse you for the transportation?"

Alice Weston, "In no way."

Later she testified, "The only money I ever received from him was from this woman with the world calendar, and it was a small expense check, I think around $20."

Once again: somebody was lying.

Under oath, I told the House Committee that Miss Weston had committed perjury and I could prove it. It was as if I was talking in an empty room. There was no response. The members couldn't have been less interested. When I first met with Casad I had been naive enough to believe the House and Senate committees were seeking truth. In fact, they wanted only to whitewash Gerald Ford in a hurry so that Jerry could pass muster as vice-president.

Here are the facts about Alice Weston. I paid Miss Weston a total of $1,000 in cash. This was in return for her introduction to Jerry Ford.

In addition, and despite her sworn testimony, I did reimburse her for her round-trip fare from Cleveland (she lived in nearby Elyria) to New York.

Among the "Weston" documents reproduced here is the letter I sent her together with a copy of the certified mail receipt.

Here also is the receipt from American Airlines for the $69.09 paid for her ticket.

Here too is a copy of a Chase Manhattan Bank Money Order for $109.25 paid to her after she submitted an expense voucher to me and several small verbal accountings.

151

Then there was another small expense voucher for which I paid her $11.30 on a First National City Bank bank check.

Again: I will be happy to take a lie detector test on this matter. My publisher has offered to pay for a similar test for Miss Weston, at her convenience.

Received from
Mr R. Winter-Berger.

$69.09 Payment
for Mrs a Schowalter
tkt # 2031029
8/25. American Airlines

THE GERALD FORD LETTERS

ART 247 R 5-63   CUSTOMER'S RECORD COPY OF—FNCB MONEY ORDER DRAWN ON

FIRST NATIONAL CITY BANK
NEW YORK

1-8
210

530948

November 4,   19 6

PAYEE   Alice Weston

SAVE
THIS
RECORD

The Remitter should sign, in ink, his or her name and address on the Money Order after filling in a date and the name of the payee. Purchaser agrees that no request for refund or to stop payment or otherwise will be made 123 East 75th St., said New York unless this customer's RECORD is submitted therewith.

PLEASE COMPLETE AND SIGN FNCB MONEY ORDER PROMPTLY

Robert Winter-Berge

123 East 75th St.

AGREEMENT
THE PURCHASER AGREES TO INSERT IN INK ON THE MONEY ORDER THE CURRENT DATE, NAME OF PAYEE AND PURCHASER'S SIGNATURE AND ADDRESS, AND TO ASSUME FULL RESPONSIBILITY FOR ALL LOSS AND LIABILITY RESULTING FROM FAILURE TO DO SO.

CUSTOMER'S COPY - PERSONAL MONEY ORDER DRAWN ON
THE CHASE MANHATTAN BANK
NATIONAL ASSOCIATION
New York, N. Y.

CM- R612319

3/17   19 67

Payee   Alice Weston

C.M.B.N.A.
-BR. 7-   109 DOLS 25 CTS

SIGNATURE   Robert Winter-Berge

ADDRESS   123 East 75" Street

SAVE THIS COPY

IMPORTANT: THE MONEY ORDER, EVEN THOUGH NOT COMPLETED, CAN BE NEGOTIATED BY ANY FINDER OR OTHER HOLDER. THEREFORE, YOU SHOULD SIGN AND COMPLETE THE MONEY ORDER AND THIS COPY PROMPTLY TO PROTECT YOURSELF AGAINST LOSS. IF MONEY ORDER IS LOST OR STOLEN, PRESENT THIS COPY AT ONCE TO THE OFFICE AT WHICH YOU OBTAINED THE MONEY ORDER. IF MONEY ORDER HAS NOT BEEN PAID, REPLACEMENT OR REFUND MAY BE MADE AND STOP ORDER ACCEPTED UPON SURRENDER OF THIS COPY OR UPON FURNISHING PROOF OF LOSS AND/OR INDEMNITY SATISFACTORY TO THE BANK.

154

123 East 75 Street
New York 21, N. Y.

August 25, 1966

My dear Alice:

Thank you so much for sending me the article
on The World Calendar which appeared in The Holland,
Michigan, Evening Sentinel on Wednesday, August 10, 1966.
I really appreciate it! This is exactly the type of
article that Jerry and myself need.

I am enclosing an open New York-Cleveland-New
York American Airline's ticket. This is little enough
payment for the aforementioned splendid article. Miss
Achelis was very happy with it.

I will be coming to Detroit in a week or so, and
would like to stop off in Cleveland to see you. Will
probably have called you before this letter arrives.

Until we speak again, I remain, with many thanks,

Yours,

Friday morning.

Dear Bob,

Any of these expenses you do not feel justified just delete.

In as much as I went to Pittsburgh solely for the World
Calendar and my visit with Jimmy Fulton as well as the
paper contacts I listed the difference involved in a stop-
over from New York which is cheaper than a direct trip back
and forth. The Philadelphia stop was in part for the Coolidges
so only listed actual expenses while there. Am charging you
for one night at the Tudor for the Look, This Week and WBB
contacts since I can only use these friends so many times.

Hope you were happy with the Chronicle Telegram article.
of
The city editor of the Cincinnati Times Star feels he can
use an article, but wants me to come down to go over it
with him. Is this worth the expense of a trip there to
you--it would run all told about $15.00?

Have not heard from Henry Erlich as yet--felt I should
wait until next week to call him.

Will be away in Nassau and Florida Nov. 20 to Dec. 1.
Would you like me to work the Florida papers? Art will
be at a convention and I will be free in the day time.

Ended up taking a cab to your place as Art got stuck in
traffic--went on directly to the airport so there was
no additional expense on your part.

Know you like bills to use so am enclosing some and you
can use them in any way you see fit.

Miss you.

Fondly,

Alice

World Calendar Expenses

Telephone Calls:

Pittsburgh	$1.25	
New York	1.10	
Cleveland	.60	
Philadelphia	1.45	
Toledo	.85	
Canton, O.	.60	
Youngstown	.35	
Akron	* .35	
	5.55	$ 6.55

Postage-------------------- 5.30

The Letter Shop 2.50

Additional expense to go to Pittsburgh plane and
limosine 11.00

hotel 10.00

Expense in New York hotel and
phone calls 12.80

cabs to make contacts 2.75

Expenses in Philadelphia Cabs 3.20

$ 54.10

*Gift to Jone Sadowski of
Chronicle Telegram*

5.15
$ 59.25

THE GERALD FORD LETTERS

THE LETTER SHOP

Mimeographing
Public Stenography
Mailings

210 Elyria Block
Elyria, Ohio
44035

Phone : FA 2-5927
Terms : Cash

Invoice No. : 66-469

October 25, 1966.

To: Mrs. Alice Schowalter
229 Hamilton Ave.
Elyria, Ohio 44035

Public Stenography - Typing letters & envelopes	2	50

1311 WESTON MASS. A. 7-12.00-1/1 1-2
OHIO   BUBS
1.45   B 045

Hotel Tudor
304 EAST 42ND STREET
NEW YORK 17, N. Y.

A 00506

MEMO.		DATE	EXPLANATION	AMT. CHARGED	AMT. CREDITED	BAL. DUE
	1	NOV-1-66	ROOM	★ 12.00		
	2	NOV-1-66	RM'TAX	★ 0.60		★ 12.60
	3	NOV-2-66	——PAID		★ 0.95	
	4	NOV-2-66	CONN. PAID		★ 0.95	
	5	NOV-2-66	CONN. PAID	(+) 0.95		
	6	NOV-2-66	——REST'R	★ 0.95		★ 12.60
	7	NOV-2-66	PAID——	★ 0.00		★ 13.55
	8	NOV-2-66	L'DIST——	★ 1.45		★ 15.00
	9	NOV-2-66	L'DIST	★ 0.62		
	10	NOV-2-66	L'DIST	★ 0.62		
	11	NOV-2-66	L'DIST	★ 0.19		★ 16.43
	12	NOV-2-66	ROOM	★ 12.00		
	13	NOV-2-66	RM'TAX	★ 0.60		★ 29.03
	14					
	15					
	16					
	17					
	18					
	19					
	20					
	21					
	22					
	23					
	24					

PAID
HOTEL TUDOR

We trust that your stay has been a
pleasant one and that we will again
have the pleasure of serving you.

NCR c167251-1

LAST BALANCE IS AMOUNT DUE
UNLESS OTHERWISE INDICATED
BILLS ARE PAYABLE WHEN PRESENTED
RETAIN THIS RECEIPT

Alice Weston,
229 Hamilton Avenue,
Elyria, Ohio.

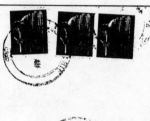

Air Mail

Mr. Robert Winter-Berger,
123 East 75th Street,
New York, N.Y. 10021

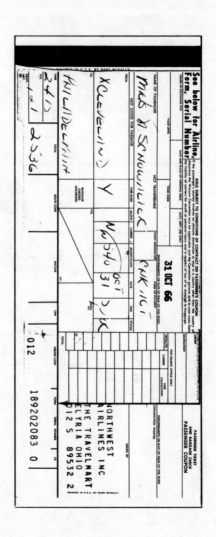

Wednesday

Dear Bob,

Last Wednesday evening was so great that life is extra dull. Bless you for arranging such a perfect evening for me.

Hope you can read this as my typewriter got knocked over and I haven't had time to get a new one. All official letters I have typed, but today it's so miserable I hate to go up to the Letter Shop.

I will type up all expenses and all contact reports tomorrow.

The gal at the Detroit Free Press was Eleanor Brightmeyer

Thank you for the check, but most of all for being such a good friend

Alice

CHAPTER SEVEN

When I began to work with Richard Casad, I was excited. He showed every symptom of really wanting to know what there was about Gerald Ford to disqualify him from receiving the vice-presidential nomination.

Was there now hope in the murky atmosphere of presidential lies and White House denials, that I, one of the corruptors, was going to throw the Nixon juggernaut off its tracks and force the president to select a more worthy man for the heart-beat-away office?

I remembered the two would-be Supreme Court appointees Nixon had made a few years before — both of whom were turned down by Congress because of information uncovered about them. I should also have remembered the words of the late Sen. Paul Douglas, who said, "Those who are tinged with sovereignty tend to think the King can do no wrong."

The first clue that something was wrong came in phone calls to me from Washington newsmen. A number of them had expressed surprise to members of Senate Rules Committee that it was planned to rule on Ford without calling me, despite the material that had appeared, unchallenged, in *The Washington Pay-Off*.

The second clue that something was wrong came from a subtle change in the direction of Casad's questions, and in his responses to what I showed and told him. He wasn't looking for reasons to discredit Ford: he wanted reasons to discredit me.

If Congress was to approve Ford's nomination, it would first have to deal with me. It would have preferred to forget me. It would have preferred that I disappear from the crust of the earth. But the persistence of the Washington press corps had forced it to where it had to go through the motions of an inquiry.

On the final day of my consultations with Casad, we were parting when I said, "Dick, they're going to nominate Ford no matter what I can show, aren't they?"

"Yes, Bob, I think so."

"Why then this exercise in futility with me?"

He didn't answer.

II

The Senate hearing has been described as a two ring circus. It wasn't. A circus is fun. My hearing

163

was a demonstration of venality. Even before I uttered my first words in closed hearings, members of the press, waiting outside, were being told I was "a liar" in my charges and that nothing I say was to be taken seriously.

Joan of Arc couldn't have faced a less friendly jury.

Sen. Robert Griffin was the most hostile. He was from Michigan, Ford's home state. He was also a longtime Ford crony.

From the beginning there were threats of prosecution for perjury. Not one of the Senators showed any willingness to examine the documents in my possession. These would have proved conclusively that previous witnesses, such as Miss Weston, had lied about a number of things.

Chairman Howard W. Cannon made not the slightest attempt to tone down the assault upon me. It was obvious that the committee members were making a concerted effort to intimidate me, and Cannon was enjoying every minute of it.

He had been chairman of the Senate Rules and Administration Committee only since the start of 1973. Though he'd been a United States senator for fifteen years, he maintained a very low profile.

His name surfaced briefly in 1964, when Riddle Airlines was fined $750 by the Civil Aeronautics Board. The fine was for providing a free flight to Las Vegas (Cannon's hometown) for a group of congressional staff members and Washington lobbyists. The purpose of the flight was to enable the passengers to attend a fund-raising dinner for Cannon.

The illegal flight came to light only as a by-product of the Robert G. ("Bobby") Baker inquiry.

Baker, who had been Lyndon Johnson's protégé and former aide, had been indicted, convicted, and jailed. In *The Washington Pay-Off* I had categorized him as one of the biggest crooks ever to operate out of an official government office.

It was obvious that no friend of Bobby Baker's was going to be a friend of mine.

Cannon appeared ready for the media. His skin was covered with an Aramis man-made tan; his hair appeared to be dyed with Clairol brown. He was a sight bordering on the comical.

By morning's end, I thought the time had come to remind him of something.

Rather than face the press in the midst of my testimony, I accepted an invitation to lunch in the office of William McWhorter Cochrane, the committee's staff director.

It was there that I encountered Cannon, face to face.

"Senator Cannon, do you recall ever meeting me?"

His eyes avoided mine. "No I don't," he said briskly, and hurried away.

He remembered me.

III

In January of 1967, Nat Voloshen asked me if I'd like to make a couple of hundred dollars.

"Sure," I'd said. "What will I have to do?"

"Would you like to fly to California for me?"

"Sure."

"But you can't stay there."

He then gave me instructions. I was to stay at the Beverly Wilshire Hotel. Sidney Korschak was to get in touch with me. Korschak, a Chicago attorney, appears to specialize in work for members of the underworld who have holdings in Las Vegas. He spends about half his time on the West Coast. He's a close friend of prominent theatrical people such as Dinah Shore and Jill St. John—both of whom I met in his company.

I had met Korschak previously in New York, when he was staying at the Hotel Carlyle, so I recognized him when he came into the lobby of the Beverly Wilshire.

We greeted each other. Then we sat in the lobby, and he gave me an envelope. "You know what to do with this," he said.

"Yes."

We chatted for a few minutes during which time he asked me how Nat was feeling. Then he went on his way, and I went to the airport to fly to Las Vegas.

In Las Vegas I was to contact Senator Cannon at the Flamingo Hotel. I phoned from the lobby.

"Senator, I'm supposed to see you. I have something for you."

"Who are you?" he asked.

"Bob Winter-Berger," I said.

"I've been expecting you," he said. "Come to my room." He gave me the room number.

He was waiting for me at the door to his room. I handed him the envelope for which he thanked me. Then I taxied back to the airport and flew to New York.

Senator Cannon said he didn't remember me. But I remembered him.

IV

The Senate Rules Committee was made up of nine members, including the chairman.

Sen. James B. Allen of Alabama was one of the most offensive. He spoke with a slow deliberate cultivated southern drawl. His questions, though low-keyed, were biased. Like Senator Cannon, he was another cosmetic wonder. A protégé of Gov. George Wallace, his viewpoints towards corruption could hardly be called liberal.

In the Winter of 1973, just before the Christmas recess, he successfully filibustered against federal funding for all general election campaigns down to the House level which would have required candidates to raise some money of their own for primary campaigns before they could become eligible for public funds.

This sorely needed reform was supported by both Republican Sen. Hugh Scott and Democrat Sen. Edward Kennedy. Although he is a Democrat, the administration supported Allen. He could hardly claim to be unbiased, and he wasn't.

He considers it a sin to say anything unflattering about this country or any of its legislators.

Senator Griffin, on the other hand, was belligerent in a loud and arrogant manner. He challenged everything I said.

I'd been in fairly good spirits when I walked into the committee room. But now, failing to heed my publisher's advice to demand either that I be permitted to tape the session or that the Senator's allow the press to observe, my initial confidence was soon replaced by frustration and despair.

To cite a clear example of the nonsense that was taking place: Griffin asked me how much I'd received in royalties for writing *The Washington Pay-Off.* (The implicit suggestion was that I, Judas, had sold out our congressional saviors for a few gold pieces.)

I told him.

He indicated that I was lying. "My information," he declared in his loud pompous voice, "is that $50,000 was paid to Mr. Winter-Berger from the Dell Publishing Company."

I assured Griffin that his information was wrong

because Dell didn't pay me directly at any time. They had a contract with my publisher to allow them to publish the paperback edition of my book. They paid my publisher, who in turn paid me my author's share of the proceeds.

Senator Griffin, who Jack Anderson exposed as having received $2,000 from Jerry Ford's own campaign funds and who admitted, when exposed, that he hadn't reported this to the chairman of the committee investigating Ford, continued to assume his holier-than-thou posture throughout.

Senator Claiborne Pell played possum throughout the hearing. He knew that with the slightest encouragement, I would discuss how I helped him to avoid both legal consequences and publicity for his arrest in a Greenwich Village gay bar.

He obviously had no desire to see that story become a part of the committee record.

When asked if he had any questions, Pell replied glumly, "Because of my knowledge of Mr. Winter-Berger's ability to fabricate, I will not ask a question at this time."

CHAPTER EIGHT

My appearance before the House Judiciary Committee was a feeble imitation of my experience before the Senate Rules Committee.

Two things were different. The Senate committee had nine members; the House committee had thirty-eight. Also, to his credit, Congressman Peter Rodino, Jr., who chaired the House proceedings, showed himself fair and impartial.

Rodino couldn't overcome the lynch mob feeling in the room. For example, Joseph J. Maraziti, a Republican congressman from New Jersey, announced in a grand manner, "It is unfortunate that this committee should be required to listen to this type of testimony, and I will not dignify the testimony of this witness by any cross-examination."

He further indicated that he thought it an outrage that anyone should be allowed to challenge the integrity of a member of Congress.

Congressman Robert Drinan, a Massachusetts Democrat, showed that party politics played no part in the hearing by hurriedly agreeing with Maraziti. He began by saying that he didn't want to appear in my next book.

The cause for the cohesive annoyance with me came to the surface when Congressman Wayne Owens, a Utah Democrat, said, "I am referring to the summary of your book, page 316, your final paragraph on that page where you say, 'Reflecting on his words, I wondered why practically every member of Congress requires a pay-off from a lobbyist before doing what he is already being well paid to do.' Is that an adequate summary ... of your attitude toward all members of Congress—that practically all of us have to be paid off before we do our duty?"

I replied, "Well, I will let the book speak for itself, sir."

Other committee members who enjoyed "liberal" reputations showed particular vexation because I had painted a "general" picture of congressmen as "gift-taking." How could I do that?

The answer was simple. They were.

Few people contribute large sums to a legislator who do not come back at some time to ask for a favor in return for their "taxed dollars" contribution. Thus the legislator is guilty of surrendering his independence for a quid pro quo. To conclude otherwise is unrealistic. The law must be changed so that no member of Congress can ever accept a gift or "contribution" or expensive "courtesy treatment" of any kind. Until this is done, lobbyists will continue to buy and sell our nation through self-serving legislation.

CHAPTER NINE

On the face of it, both committee hearings were savage attacks on my credibility. However on examination of the actual questions and answers, it becomes evident that the thrust was to dishonor me and to head off any documentary material I had to support what I had written and said.

The case of Francis Leonard Kellogg was gone into in some detail in *The Washington Pay-Off*. Here are the facts as I know them and despite the compulsion of everybody concerned to "deny everything" and to cloud the chronology.

Kellogg was a client of mine for whom Jerry Ford did intensive work.

Kellogg was the president and a major stockholder of the International Mining Company in New York. Although only in his fifties, he wanted to retire. On the other hand, he didn't want to just sit around in his living room and stare at a television set.

Kellogg told me he had an income of about $150,000 a year. His wife, a Wanamaker and a Munn, had an even larger independent income. The

Kelloggs, who were subsequently divorced, weren't worrying about needing coffee and cake money.

One reason Kellogg wanted a job in government was to have an excuse to get rid of all of his International Mining stock to avoid a conflict of interest. The stock was currently selling at a historically high price, and Kellogg felt it was a good time to sell out.

He loved big-game hunting. He spent several weeks a year at it in Africa. He owned a fifteen thousand acre ranch in Kenya, and he'd been there so often that he could speak Kiswahili.

Kellogg decided that it would be a lot of fun for him to become the United States ambassador to Kenya.

II

I met Mr. Kellogg through Gus Ober, the same Gus Ober who had introduced me to Claiborne Pell.

My agreement with Kellogg called for me to shepherd him to the ambassadorship through my close friendship with Gerald Ford.

At the time, I thought I might like to work for Kellogg's company. I decided to volunteer my "talent" and hope that I would be repaid in kind.

Kellogg agreed to pay my expenses. These came to about $950.

I will not bore the reader with the details of the entire strategy and action except in skeletal form.

III

I asked Jerry Ford if he would see Kellogg. I told him that Kellogg was a lifelong Republican and had contributed $30,000 to the 1968 Nixon campaign through Maurice Stans in New York.

I added that Kellogg wanted very much to be considered for the post of ambassador to Kenya.

"That's his first preference," I added.

Ford said that he didn't have time. About his contribution he said, "That's in New York. Why doesn't he go to his own state Republicans?"

"Because Javits and Goodell don't have much clout with the president," I explained. "True, we need Javits and Goodell because they could block an appointment. But he has to get to the president and since you're such a good friend of the president's, I wish you could see him."

Ford repeated, "Bob, I just don't have the time."

I gave him Kellogg's social and financial background, but that didn't move him. I then said, "He will guarantee $30,000 to the Congressional Boosters Club in ten equal payments."

That did it.

Ford replied, "On your way out, speak to Mildred about an appointment. I'll be happy to see him at any time convenient to you and him."

That was the beginning of the Kellogg campaign.
The Kellogg-Ford meeting took place in February
of 1969.

IV

At the first meeting, Kellogg gave Ford a check
made out to the Republican Congressional Boosters
Club for $3,000.

The club is set up to fund the campaigns of
incumbent congressmen as well as men running for
office for the first time. A contribution made this
way would get Jerry his "brownie" points. Then, if
he needed money for his campaign or for the
campaign of some newcomer he wanted to encour-
age, the odds were excellent that he could have it.

I was present at the first meeting. It lasted about
twenty minutes.

In a sworn affidavit, furnished to the Senate Rules
Committee, Kellogg said that he had three meetings
with Ford, all of them brief. He denied that there
had been any discussion of contributions at the first
meeting.

I don't know if Kellogg kept his pledge on the
balance of the $30,000, but I do know that he made
at least one additional contribution. In a letter dated
September 22, Ford wrote:

Dear Fran:

Just a note to thank you again for your very
generous contribution to the Republican Congres-

sional Boosters Club. I have sent your check on to Congressman Bob Wilson, who is Chairman of the Republican Congressional Committee.

Thank you again and very best wishes.

It was signed, Jerry.

V

Every second or third time that I saw Jerry Ford, I inquired about the progress of the Kellogg case.

In his affidavit, Kellogg says "Insofar as I'm aware, apart from favorable recommendations, Congressman Ford had nothing to do with my appointment to my present position."

The "present position" referred to was not ambassador to Kenya. Kellogg had to settle for the job as the State Department's "Special Assistant to the Secretary for Refugees and Migration."

Kellogg has the rank of ambassador. He's special assistant to the secretary of state.

Jerry Ford did it for him.

Here are a few of the letters written by the man who swore in an affidavit that he didn't know that Ford was responsible for getting him his job and that he had only three brief meetings with Ford.

INTERNATIONAL MINING CORPORATION
280 PARK AVENUE
NEW YORK, N.Y. 10017

F. L. KELLOGG
PRESIDENT

February 19, 1969

Dear Clay:

It was thoughtful of you, as always, to call before departing for Europe.

Herewith a condensed progress report.

I have seen:

Senator Jacob Javits. He took notes, my biography, and implied Kenya might be easier to get than the Arts Foundation.

Ambassador Philip Crowe. Excellent advice; a fine letter to Secretary Rogers.

Secretary Maurice Stans. One brief letter to me. Silence.

Elmer Bobst. I have an appointment in Palm Beach this weekend.

Ambassador William Attwood. Tremendous enthusiasm for Kenya; three marvelous letters.

Congressman Gerald Ford. Appointment in Washington, February 25, to ask his advice.

Through friends:

Charles Ill (on Nixon's screening committee) through Arnie Gay. My biography and letter delivered by hand February 12. On February 18, he reported my file on Harry Fleming's desk.

Peter Flanagan (on Nixon's screening committee) through Ernest Byfield. Biography and letter sent at his request.

My contacts:

Langhorne Washburn (Republican Finance Committee). Biography and covering letter mailed February 14.

'Bus' Mosbacher (Protocol). Sent biography and acknowledgment received. Through him I have requested an appointment with Secretary Rogers or Under Secretary Richardson.

Dan Hofgren (Deputy Assistant to the President). In constant contact. Have kept him fully informed.

Letters in addition to the above:

Lauson H. Stone to Secretary Rogers.

Russell E. Train to Under Secretary Richardson.

Letters to be requested:

Secretary Dillon Ripley	Mr. Kermit Roosevelt
Senator Jacob K. Javits	Mr. Harold Coolidge
General Charles Lindbergh	Mr. John Hanes
Mr. Livingston L. Biddle	Mr. John Olin
Mr. Gardner Cowles	Mr. Kenneth Keating

What about Angier Duke, Tony Akers, William McCormick Blair--all friends-- but all Democrats?

And John Millar and Robert McBride in the State Department?

Also on my list:

Mr. Jeremiah Milbank	Mr. Thomas Dewey
Mr. David Rockefeller	Mr. Brownie Reed
Mr. Hobart Lewis	Mr. William Paley
Senator Charles E. Goodell	Mrs. Helen Frick
Mr. Lowell Thomas	

I hope to see you in Washington this Tuesday, February 25. Your advice and counsel would be enormously helpful.

With great warmth and affection for all the Pells,

Yours,

FLK/nc   F. L. Kellogg

The Honorable Claiborne Pell
3425 Prospect Street
Washington, D. C.
bc: Mr. Robert N. Winter-Berger

March 9, 1969

The President
The White House
Washington, D. C.

Mr. President:

In February three years ago arrangements were made by me
through Mr. Langhorne Washburn for a luncheon meeting of
the National Republican Boosters Association, at which you
were the Guest of Honor, here in Palm Beach. I had the
pleasure of acting as Chairman of the meeting, introducing
the local Republican Congressmen who were present and
Mr. Gerald Ford, Minority Leader of the House and, finally,
yourself.

Of course I am happy to have been one of the first to
support your candidacy when the organization began in
California two years ago.

The purpose of this letter is to urge the appointment of a
very qualified man, and close friend of mine, as Ambassador
to Kenya, East Africa, Mr. Francis L. Kellogg, of Palm
Beach and New York, President of International Mining Corporation. He and his family have spent part of each year
in Kenya for approximately nine years. He and his wife
own a larg farm and have been active in the affairs in
Kenya and are well known there. Mr. Kellogg, as a Director
of the World Wild Life Fund and donor of the Louwana Fund,
has been active in the conservation of African wild life.

He is well known for his charm and managing ability. I
believe he is uniquely qualified to serve his country as
Ambassador to Kenya and I think his appointment would be
appreciated by the many people who know him in Kenya.

Respectfully,

Walter S. Gubelmann

WHG:amr

INTERNATIONAL MINING CORPORATION
280 PARK AVENUE
NEW YORK, N.Y. 10017

F. L. KELLOGG
PRESIDENT

March 26, 1969

Mr. Jack A. Gleason
Assistant to the Secretary
U. S. Department of Commerce
Washington, D.C. 20230

Dear Mr. Gleason:

I did want you to know that I am deeply appreciative of my two very constructive telephone conversations with you. At least I have some compass bearings as to where I am!

As you know, I believe I could serve my country and my party best in Kenya because of my family's long association with that country, my understanding of its politics, economic problems, and my awareness of the sensitivity of the post. However, I now understand that there is another candidate for this assignment and that my chances are thereby considerably diminished.

Alternatively, the position of Assistant Secretary of State for Education and Cultural Affairs is presently unfilled and several friends including Dillon Ripley, and Congressmen Gerald Ford and Seymour Halpern, among others, have recommended me for this position and both Senators Javits and Goodell are aware of these aspirations. I have discussed the responsibilities and duties of this important role with officials in State and with former incumbents and believe I am well qualified by reason of wide administrative experience to fill this post.

Today I learned that there is at least one other contender under consideration. As a consequence, it is imperative for me to enlist the active support and endorsement of your office if my candidacy is to be successful. Therefore, I hope I can count on your support and recommendation for my appointment as Assistant Secretary of State for Education and Cultural Affairs.

Very truly yours,

F. L. Kellogg

FLK/nc

bc: Mr. Robert N. Winter-Berger

INTERNATIONAL MINING CORPORATION
280 PARK AVENUE
NEW YORK, N.Y. 10017

F. L. KELLOGG
PRESIDENT

May 28, 1969

Mr. Peter Flanigan
The White House
1600 Pennsylvania Avenue
Washington, D. C.

Dear Mr. Flanigan:

I greatly appreciated your kind candor in our meeting last week and I understand the current situation as you outlined it.

I remain enthusiastic about serving this Administration, preferably in the Foreign Service area for which I believe my experience in international business affairs involving knowledge of foreign countries, diplomacy, economic conditions, and familiarity with local customs and practices has particularly fitted me. As you know, for the past ten years I have also served three international agencies whose activities are largely abroad: International Rescue Committee, World Wildlife Fund and Louwana Fund.

Following your suggestion, I would like to be considered in the future for any of the Mediterranean countries, such as Morocco, Tunisia, Malta, or for the Caribbean (Barbados, Jamaica, Trinidad). Of course, a special or roving assignment would be of great interest.

In the meantime I am continuing to investigate other possibilities for service within Government which, hopefully, may cause our paths to cross again.

Appreciatively,

F. L. Kellogg

FLK/nc

JOHN J. ROONEY
MEMBER OF CONGRESS
14TH DISTRICT, NEW YORK

SUITE 2268
RAYBURN OFFICE BUILDING
WASHINGTON, D.C. 20515

MEMBER
COMMITTEE ON APPROPRIATIONS

Congress of the United States
House of Representatives
Washington, D. C.

CHAIRMAN
SUBCOMMITTEE ON
APPROPRIATIONS:
STATE
JUSTICE
COMMERCE
JUDICIARY AND
RELATED AGENCIES
MEMBER:
FOREIGN OPERATIONS

April 17, 1969

Mr. F. L. Kellogg
President
International Mining Corporation
280 Park Avenue
New York, New York 10017

Dear Mr. Kellogg:

In reply to your letter of the 14th instant
and because of your friendship with my friend Angie Duke,
as well as the occasion at the River Club, I hasten to be
utterly frank with you. I would recommend strongly that
you have nothing to do with the position titled, "Assistant
Secretary of State for Education and Cultural Affairs."
Believe me, you can't win in that job, and would only
have a seven day a week headache.

With kindest regards,

Sincerely,

[signature]

JJR:sls

THE GERALD FORD LETTERS

INTERNATIONAL MINING CORPORATION
280 PARK AVENUE • NEW YORK, N.Y. 10017

F. L. KELLOGG
PRESIDENT

April 28, 1969

The Honorable Gerald R. Ford
House of Representatives
Office of the Minority Leader
H. 230
Washington, D.C.

Dear Congressman Ford:

Thank you for your continued interest and efforts in my behalf.

I had a lengthy and most friendly discussion by telephone with
Senator Javits here today, and I have every reason to believe I
have secured exactly "the push" you suggested was necessary.

Very truly yours,

F. L. Kellogg

FLK/nc
Blind photocopy: Mr. Robert N. Winter-Berger

INTERNATIONAL MINING CORPORATION
280 PARK AVENUE
NEW YORK, N.Y. 10017

F. L. KELLOGG
PRESIDENT

May 2, 1969

The Honorable Stanley Blair
Assistant to Vice President Agnew
Room 276
Executive Office Building
Washington, D. C.

My dear Mr. Blair:

I think the following advice received this morning from my friend Ambassador Angier Biddle Duke is important enough to communicate to you:

***"Naturally, the post that interests me most for you and for which I think you would be admirably suited is our Embassy in Kenya. I don't think you should be too discouraged by your conversation with Wilmot Hastings. In reading Newsweek today it would appear that our mutual friend, Peter Flanigan, is a decisive factor in the appointments field and it might be very useful to talk the situation over with him.

"As for the post of Assistant Secretary for Education and Cultural Affairs, I honestly don't believe it is worth pursuing. If I were you I would get to either Senator Javits or Senator Goodell, or both, and be specific in your zeroing in on the post in Kenya as an example of your desire for public service. The last Ambassador there was not a career man and therefore, there is a perfectly good precedent in such an appointment, and his predecessor, Bill Attwood, also was a political appointee."***

As you know, the post in Kenya has been my first preference from the outset. Anything that you can do will be, I can assure you, very greatly appreciated (particularly since I know that Vice President Agnew has a candidate of his own for the Assistant Secretaryship).

Very truly yours,

F. L. Kellogg

FLK/nc

Blind photocopy: Mr. Robert N. Winter-Berger

INTERNATIONAL MINING CORPORATION
280 PARK AVENUE
NEW YORK, N.Y. 10017

F. L. KELLOGG
PRESIDENT

May 2, 1969

The Honorable Gerald R. Ford
Office of the Minority Leader
House of Representatives
Washington, D. C. 20515

My dear Congressman Ford:

I think the following advice received this morning from my friend Ambassador Angier Biddle Duke is important enough to communicate to you:

***"Naturally, the post that interests me most for you and for which I think you would be admirably suited is our Embassy in Kenya. I don't think you should be too discouraged by your conversation with Wilmot Hastings. In reading Newsweek today it would appear that our mutual friend, Peter Flanigan, is a decisive factor in the appointments field and it might be very useful to talk the situation over with him.

"As for the post of Assistant Secretary for Education and Cultural Affairs, I honestly don't believe it is worth pursuing. If I were you I would get to either Senator Javits or Senator Goodell, or both, and be specific in zeroing in on the post in Kenya as an example of your desire for public service. The last Ambassador there was not a career man and therefore, there is a perfectly good precedent in such an appointment and his predecessor, Bill Attwood, also was a political appointee."***

As you know, I have been in touch personally with Senator Javits who has promised to reactivate my application today in Washington.

Very truly yours,

F. L. Kellogg

FLK/nc

Blind photocopy: Mr. Robert N. Winter-Berger

THE GERALD FORD LETTERS

INTERNATIONAL MINING CORPORATION
280 PARK AVENUE
NEW YORK, N.Y. 10017

F. L. KELLOGG
PRESIDENT

May 20, 1969

Mrs. Elly M. Peterson
Republican National Committee
1625 Eye Street
Washington, D. C.   20006

Dear Mrs. Peterson:

It was a great pleasure to talk with you by telephone yesterday and a relief to have positive news about the post in Kenya--even if bad--after four months of vacuum.

I will be enormously appreciative if you can find out if the Assistant Secretary-ship for Education and Cultural Affairs is available. If not, I have been advised to give you a number of alternatives:

>   FIRST: TUNISIA
>
>   SECOND: MOROCCO
>
>   THIRD: BARBADOS

I will be glad to write you briefly as to my international experience and qualifications in both business and other areas in connection with these positions if it would be helpful.

Very truly yours,

F. L. Kellogg

FLK/nc

INTERNATIONAL MINING CORPORATION

280 PARK AVENUE · NEW YORK, N.Y. 10017

F. L. KELLOGG
PRESIDENT

May 28, 1969

The Honorable Gerald R. Ford
Minority Leader
House of Representatives
Capitol H. 230
Washington, D. C.

Dear Gerry:

Attached is a copy of my letter to Peter Flanigan following my
interview with him last Thursday. I was told I was among the
60 who were approved as qualified but for whom there were
only 27 non-career positions. As for Kenya, State decided
this should be filled by a professional as internal strife and
possibly civil war may follow Kenyatta's death.

I remain confident that something ultimately will develop.

In the meantime, if you have any plans to be in New York, we
would like to have you and Mrs. Ford for dinner with friends
who share mutual interests. Please let me know.

Warmest regards,

F. L. Kellogg

FLK/nc

INTERNATIONAL MINING CORPORATION
280 PARK AVENUE
NEW YORK, N.Y. 10017

F. L. KELLOGG
PRESIDENT

June 23, 1969

Mr. Peter Flanigan
The White House
1600 Pennsylvania Avenue
Washington, D. C.

Dear Mr. Flanigan:

I am writing you at the suggestion of Congressman Gerald R. Ford, who has told me that my name is among those being considered for the position of U. S. Representative on the Trusteeship Council. I am intensely interested in receiving favorable consideration for this assignment and believe that I am qualified to carry out the duties and responsibilities of the post.

For your information, because the U. S. Mission (Personnel Division) does not have a job description for this Presidential appointment, I have arranged for an interview with Ambassador Charles Yost this week to discuss the position and hopefully to secure his assent to my candidacy.

As you already know, the last twenty years have provided me with an exceptionally broad business background with particular emphasis on foreign operations. International Mining has been extremely active in Canada, Australia, Mexico, and South America, which has required an intimate knowledge of foreign politics and economics, as well as an innate sense of diplomacy.

In addition to this exposure to foreign affairs, I have been extremely active for the past ten years in civic and philanthropic organizations which operate principally overseas. Of these, International Rescue Committee, of which I am a director and vice president, is probably the best known. It has aided countless thousands of refugees escape political tyranny, as well as providing emergency relief, medical assistance, etc., for the displaced.

American Immigration and Citizenship Conference is concerned with immigration to the U. S. and related activities, such as the world refugee problem. It coordinates the efforts of more than 90 leading civic, religious, educational, labor and social welfare agencies in this field in which it is probably the single-most important force. I have served as a director and officer (treasurer) since 1961.

Mr. Peter Flanigan   -2-   June 23, 1969

About ten years ago I was also elected to the Boards of two conservation organizations, World Wildlife Fund and Louwana Fund. Both constantly deal on the highest levels with governmental representatives of many countries and have brought me wide experience in working abroad.

In conclusion, I have travelled extensively, particularly to African countries where political events and economic trends have been followed with keen interest.

I therefore feel well qualified by reason of education, experience, and mature judgment to fill the requirements of the Trusteeship Council position, an assignment in which I am most deeply interested.

Very truly yours,

F. L. Kellogg

FLK/nc

INTERNATIONAL MINING CORPORATION
280 PARK AVENUE
NEW YORK, N.Y. 10017

F. L. KELLOGG
PRESIDENT

June 26, 1969

The Honorable Emil Mosbacher
Chief of Protocol
Department of State
2201 C Street
Washington, D. C.

Dear Bus:

You were most considerate to give all my family a lift to the White House this last Tuesday.

Attached is a copy of my letter to Peter Flanigan for your information. I had a pleasant and constructive interview with Ambassador Yost today and the way is clear for the U. N. position if the White House approves. I have the endorsement of Messrs. Gerald Ford, Javits, Goodell and Halpern, so am hopeful of success, but I know a word from you would be of tremendous help.

Appreciatively,

F. L. Kellogg

FLK/nc
Enclosure

Bob —
in case you

Compliments of

FRANK L. KELLOGG

missed this

PRESIDENT
INTERNATIONAL MINING CORPORATION

5 AMBASSADORSHIPS FILLED BY PRESIDENT

SAN CLEMENTE, Calif., Aug. 20 (AP)—President Nixon filed five ambassadorial posts today, including the one in Rome. A career diplomat, Graham A. Martin of Thomasville, N. C., was named Ambassador to Italy.

Douglas MacArthur 2d of Washington, a nephew of Gen. Douglas MacArthur, is being shifted from his current post in Austria to be Ambassador to Iran.

Vincent de Roulet, mayor of the village of North Hills, L. I., was named Ambassador to Jamaica.

Robinson McIlvaine of Downington, Pa., one of the State Department's leading authorities on African affairs and now Ambassador to Guinea, is being transferred to the East African republic of Kenya.

John Partick Walsh, a career Foreign Service officer from Chicago, will be Ambassador to Kuwait.

Mr. Martin, who is 56 years old, has served more than 20 years in the Foreign Service. He will succeed Ambassador Gardner Ackley, who is leaving Government service.

Mr. Martin has been special assistant to the Secretary of State for Refugee and Migration Affairs.

NY
Times
Aug 21

191

Bob — for "your eyes only"
F

DIARY OF A WOULD-BE
POLITICAL APPOINTEE

Wednesday   9:00 P.M. Shuttle to Washington
(9/17/69)
                Takes off at 10:35 P.M. on account of electrical storm
                Lands at Dulles instead of National
                Arrive at Senator Pell's at 12:45 A.M.

Thursday   9:30 A.M. Congressman Ford's office
(9/18/69)
                Review of 'case history'. Gerry promises to look into availabili*
                of the U.S. Representative on the U.N. Trusteeship Council.

                Join the Republican Congressional Boosters Club.

                10:25 A.M. Senator Pell's office

                Greet all the staff (my daughter worked a summer here) and use
                Claiborne's 'phone.

                10:45 A.M. Senator Javits' office

                Review 'case history' with Jean McKey who coordinates the
                Senator's political appointments with Senator Goodell. She
                promises continued support.

                11:30 A.M. Senator Goodell's office

                Review 'case history' with the Senator and his Administrative
                Assistant, John Grant. Charlie promises to 'phone Peter Flanig
                on my behalf.

                12:10 P.M. Congressman Ogden Reid's office

                Review 'case history'. Am informed that a meeting took place th
                morning between Peter Flanigan and Elliot Richardson re this jol
                Reid states there is a list of fifteen candidates for this appointme
                two from New York State, but that a third has the edge. He is
                very negative about my chances.

                12:45 P.M. Lunch at the Jockey Club

DIARY OF A WOULD-BE
POLITICAL APPOINTEE

-2-

hursday
ont'd.)

2:30 P. M. Request to see Ambassador Mosbacher

Negative. He is at the U. N. with the President.

2:45 P. M. Wilmot Hastings' office (Special Assistant to Under
Secretary of State)

Review 'case history'. Informed that there are several candidates but that Senator Karl Mundt's protege has the edge and is
undergoing a 'security check'. He says there are, if any, few
Presidential appointments left. Can only suggest appropriate
Congressional Foreign Investigative Commission of which there
are 588 scheduled for 1970.

3:30 P. M. Congressman Rogers Morton's office

Review 'case history'. He states existence of Senator Mundt's
protege is news to him and that he will check. He can't understand any interest on the part of a South Dakotan in this position
and he speaks of the importance of the post, especially vis-a-
vis the Russians.

I report that I have joined the Republican Congressional Boosters
and as I leave he promises to do 'something'.

4:10 P. M. Stanley Blair's office (Assistant to the Vice President)

Review 'case history'. He regrets I was unable to see the Vice
President the previous day and I explain the conflict with IMC's
Board Meeting. A new appointment is being scheduled. Stanley
agrees the outlook for the U. N. position not encouraging but
promises to call Peter Flanigan. He agrees that perhaps the
best plan is to be patient and wait until an appointive position
opens.

5:25 P. M. Shuttle to New York (Second Section.)

GERALD R. FORD
FIFTH DISTRICT, MICHIGAN

MICHIGAN OFFICE
425 CHERRY STREET S
GRAND RAPIDS
ZIP 49502

Congress of the United States
Office of the Minority Leader
House of Representatives
Washington, D.C. 20515

September 22, 1969

Mr. Francis L. Kellogg
International Mining Corporation
280 Park Avenue
New York, New York 10017

Dear Fran:

Just a note to again thank you for the very generous
contribution to the Republican Congressional Boosters
Club. I have sent your check on to Congressman Bob
Wilson who is Chairmam of the Republican Congressional
Committee.

Thank you again and very best wishes.

Sincerely,

Gerald R. Ford, M. C.

GRF:1

194

INTERNATIONAL MINING CORPORATION

280 PARK AVENUE · NEW YORK, N.Y. 10017

F. L. KELLOGG
PRESIDENT

October 9, 1969

Mr. Jeremiah Milbank
Republican National Finance Committee
1625 Eye Street, N. W.
Washington, D. C. 20006

Dear Jerry:

I accept your invitation to join the Republican National Finance Committee
and in due course hope to learn more about its membership and how it is
organized in relationship to the other committees.

In the meantime, I have already heard from Frederick Ehrman, Chairman
in New York, who tells me the first meeting is scheduled for 4:30, Tuesday,
October 21, at the Sky Club. I look forward to seeing you at that time.

Very truly yours,

F. L. Kellogg

FLK/nc

P.S.   I attach the latest on my own Government pursuit.

F. L. K.

bc: Mr. Robert N. Winter-Berger

THE GERALD FORD LETTERS

INTERNATIONAL MINING CORPORATION
280 PARK AVENUE · NEW YORK, N.Y. 10017

F. L. KELLOGG
PRESIDENT

November 3, 1969

The Honorable Gerald R. Ford
Office of the Minority Leader
House of Representatives
Washington, D. C.   20515

Dear Gerry:

I have studied the "Schedule of International Conferences" which you sent me
with great interest.

Several of these seem to be within my sphere which as you know encompasses
general business administration, mining activities, and social problems, such
as refugees and immigration, and I have long been concerned with the African
situation as a result in part of a number of trips to North and East Africa over
the last ten years.

Therefore, of the International Conferences scheduled for the next three months,
the particular session which I believe I can contribute the most towards is:

UNESCO Regional Conference of Ministers of Education and Ministers
Responsible for Economic Planning in the Arab States

According to the schedule, the meeting is scheduled from January 5 to January
16 in Morocco. If it can be arranged for me to join the U.S. representatives,
I do not believe there will be any problem at International Mining Corporation.

On Thursday, November 6th, I have a 3:45 p.m. appointment with Vice President
Agnew. Could I have no more than ten minutes on that same day with you?
11:30 a.m. would be perfect if your schedule permits, but, of course, another
time can be arranged if it suits you better. I will call Miss Leonard this Wednesday to see if a meeting is possible.

Very truly yours,

F. L. Kellogg

FLK/nc

bc: Mr. Robert N. Winter-Berger

196

INTERNATIONAL MINING CORPORATION

280 PARK AVENUE • NEW YORK, N.Y. 10017

. L. KELLOGG
PRESIDENT

November 24, 1969

The Honorable Gerald R. Ford
Office of the Minority Leader
House of Representatives
Washington, D. C.   20515

Dear Gerry:

I learned from the State Department Friday that the announcement of the appointment of Senator Mundt's candidate to the U. N. Trusteeship Council is imminent.

During my meeting with Vice President Agnew on November 6, I asked his help to secure the position of "U. S. Representative to the U. S. Mission to the European Community in Brussels" presently held by a career appointee of former Vice President Humphrey.

Since then I have learned that the "Special Assistant to the Secretary for Refugees and Migration" is vacant. Having been closely involved in this area for ten years or more as an officer and director of International Rescue Committee and as a member of the Executive Committee and treasurer of American Immigration and Citizenship Conference, I feel I am particularly qualified to serve in this tough and sensitive post.

At this moment, however, Ambassador Martin, the former incumbent, and the President have offered this position to a close friend of the President's. If he should decline, I hope I can count again on your strong endorsement for that State Department job.

I will be in Washington, Tuesday, December 2, to be briefed for the January "Conference of Ministers Responsible for Economic Planning in the Arab States" and plan to stop by your office briefly during the afternoon. If you are unavailable, I will, of course, fully understand.

Very truly yours,

F. L. Kellogg

FLK/nc

INTERNATIONAL MINING CORPORATION

280 PARK AVENUE · NEW YORK, N.Y. 10017

F. L. KELLOGG
PRESIDENT

December 8, 1969

Dr. Ray Page
Superintendent of Public Instruction
State of Illinois
State Office Building
Springfield, Illinois 62706

Dear Ray:

I found our "briefing sessions" at the Department of State last Tuesday of great
interest, and, for your convenience, I attach a copy of the names and titles of
some of those present.

Obvious omissions on this list are:

> Dr. Pardee Lowe, Education Officer
> Office of Multilateral Policy and Programs
> Bureau of Educational and Cultural Affairs
> Department of State
> Washington, D. C.

and

> Miss Annis Sandvos, Deputy Director
> Office of Multilateral Policy and Programs
> Bureau of Educational and Cultural Affairs

Also enclosed is a copy of my travel schedule.

If you and I agree to submit a written report on the Conference, perhaps it should
be prefaced by a comment about the "briefing sessions?" This would be, I believe, a departure from previous reports.

I look forward to the Conference and to meeting you again, Sunday evening,
January 11, at the Mamounia Hotel, when the Charge d'Affaires for the U. S.
Embassy in Rabat is scheduled to be present.

Very truly yours,

F. L. Kellogg

FLK/nc
Enclosures

bc: Mr. Robert N. Winter-Berger

VI

Time Magazine on December 3, 1973, noted that Herbert Kalmbach was "the President's personal attorney and a key Nixon money man." It was shown that Kalmbach had asked The Associated Milk Producers, Inc. to make a cash contribution to Kalmbach. $100,000 was delivered. The money was supposedly added to a 1968 Nixon campaign surplus and "was eventually used for a variety of purposes."

In *The Washington Pay-Off* I said, in response to Kellogg's persistent request to introduce me to Waller Taylor, the president's former law partner, whom he had heard about:

"We walked over to Kellogg's office. Kellogg had heard about Waller Taylor from de Roulet (Vincent de Roulet), and so he was impressed by an unexpected visit from such a notable personage. After listening to Kellogg's tale of woe, Taylor said the only way to get the appointment (an ambassadorship) was to get the ear of President Nixon and his personal aide Peter Flanigan, both of whom Waller said were his close friends. Taylor said that he would be happy to try for Kellogg but that he would need a cash payment of $65,000 to take care of his time and the needs of both Nixon and Flanigan. Kellogg agreed to have the money for Taylor that afternoon, and we arranged a meeting for later in the day in Kellogg's office."

Kellogg denied under oath that he ever gave

WALLER TAYLOR II
1035 PACIFIC MUTUAL BUILDING
523 WEST SIXTH STREET
LOS ANGELES, CALIFORNIA 90014

February 7, 1969

Dear Bob:

Thanks so very much for your extremely courteous note. I feel remiss in not having written to thank you for taking such excellent care of Elizabeth during our visit in Washington.

I deeply regret the fact that we did not have an opportunity to see you before we left and that the exodus from the Sheraton-Park was so miserable. I did call Elizabeth when we finally got to the Hotel, however, and determined that you had all returned safely.

Again let me tell you what a pleasure it was having had the opportunity of meeting and visiting with you. I will certainly let you know the next time I am in New York, and, hopefully, we can get together for a visit.

Both Jane and I are extremely appreciative of your offer to take Steve to Washington. As I told you, I think it would be a marvelous opportunity for him, as I know he does. You are indeed most kind to take such an interest in him.

Thanks again, and with kindest personal regards.

Sincerely,

Waller

THE GERALD FORD LETTERS

INTERNATIONAL MINING CORPORATION

280 PARK AVENUE · NEW YORK, N.Y. 10017

L. KELLOGG
PRESIDENT

May 28, 1969

Mr. Waller Taylor, 2nd
523 West Sixth Street
Los Angeles 14, California

Dear Waller:

I believe Bob has relayed to you the abortive results of my last
week's meeting with Peter Flanigan, which are confirmed by the
copy of my letter to him to the White House.

I was told I was among the 60 who were approved as qualified
but for whom there were only 27 non-career positions. As for
Kenya, State decided this should be filled by a professional as
internal strife and possibly civil war may follow Kenyatta's
death.

If you were able to put in a 'good word' for me either with Peter
or his boss, I am most appreciative. Something may still develop
and, in any event, (being of Scottish extraction) I never give up!

If you didn't get a chance to call Flanigan maybe you still could
to find out his reaction to the interview?

I greatly enjoyed our meeting and I'm certain our paths will cross
somewhere between here and California in the not too distant
future.

Warmest regards,

F. L. Kellogg

FLK/nc

201

bc: Mr. Robert N. Winter-Berger

INTERNATIONAL MINING CORPORATION
280 PARK AVENUE
NEW YORK, N.Y. 10017

F. L. KELLOGG
PRESIDENT

August 11, 1969

Mr. Herbert W. Kalmbach
550 Newport Centre Drive, Suite 900
Newport Beach, California   92660

Dear Mr. Kalmbach:

I very much appreciated the time and interest you took in calling me last Friday.

My initial objective was to serve this Administration in Kenya, a country I know well and have visited many times. However, in May Mr. Peter Flanigan explained the valid reasons why State desired to appoint a career professional to this post.

Subsequently, I have sought the appointment as U.S. Representative on the U.N. Trusteeship Council which has been vacant for some months. In this connection I have been interviewed by Ambassador Charles Yost and believe I can count on his endorsement.

Many friends have written letters in my behalf to the President, the Secretary, and top officials at State and to the White House staff. I know Mr. Maurice Stans and am also known and have the endorsement of Senators Javits and Goodell and Congressmen Gerald Ford, Rogers Morton and Seymour Halpern, all of whom are familiar with my aspiration to serve this Administration. Dan Hofgren (Deputy Assistant to the President), Lang Washburn (at Commerce), Stanley Blair (Assistant to the Vice President) are all friends and have been very helpful but my campaign is in its eighth month and still unsuccessful.

I could enclose copies of many letters but in the interest of brevity attach just a representative selection plus my biography. Believe me, your assistance is very greatly appreciated. I could come out to California if you thought it propitious.

Very truly yours,

F. L. Kellogg

FLK/nc
Enclosures

P.S. You undoubtedly know Waller Taylor, who can give you his opinion as to my ability and personality.

F. L. K.

INTERNATIONAL MINING CORPORATION
280 PARK AVENUE
NEW YORK, N.Y. 10017

L. KELLOGG
PRESIDENT

November 25, 1969

Waller Taylor, 2nd, Esq.
Adams, Duque & Haseltine
523 West Sixth Street
Los Angeles, California 90014

Dear Waller:

It's a long time since we touched base--hence this note, together
with the latest two letters to Washington which will bring you up-
to-date.

Very little progress to report, as you can see. I think the only
end of road blocks is through a meeting with the President.

Could you possibly consider arranging this in my behalf?

Yours very truly,

F. L. Kellogg

FLK/nc
Enclosures

bc: Mr. Robert Winter-Berger

Taylor any money. Yet, Kalmbach was also soon in touch with Kellogg. One must keep in mind that Kalmbach was supposedly only the president's personal counsel. He had no official government status. In theory, he had no power to get a job for anyone.

The facts, as the Watergate investigations showed, were that virtually everything in government was for sale, if the sellers were one of that group of bribe-takers and power-manipulators in the intimate Nixon circles.

CHAPTER TEN

Jerry Ford, better known as "honest Gerald Ford," has said that he wrote to me "only a half a dozen letters" (Jack Anderson, July 20, 1972).

So far, dear reader, you have had the opportunity to examine fourteen letters to me from Ford, and a number of others from Ford to my clients, with copies to me.

Here is another sampling. I'll include the other correspondence related to these too. Note the "warmest personal regards" from Jerry to me. Note the reference to "your good friend Jerry Ford," by the chairman of the Kent County (Michigan) Republican Finance Committee. And recall Jerry's spontaneous remarks to a large audience in front of Richard Nixon in which he named me as his good friend to whom he felt a sense of appreciation.

GERALD R. FORD
FIFTH DISTRICT, MICHIGAN

MICHIGAN OFFICE:
425 CHERRY STREET SE
GRAND RAPIDS

Congress of the United States
Office of the Minority Leader
House of Representatives
Washington, D.C.

September 23, 1966

Mr. Robert N. Winter-Berger
123 East 75th Street
New York, New York 10021

Dear Bob:

Many, many thanks for your wonderful help for the Republican
Legislative Dinner. Mildred has told me that you plan additional
assistance to the effort, and believe me I am deeply grateful.

At this point my schedule in the mornings next week doesn't look
too hectic. (As you know however, this can change in a matter of
seconds) But if you will give the office a call on Monday or
Tuesday, I am sure a mutually convenient time can be worked out
when we can chat a bit.

Once again, thanks a million and warmest personal regards.

Sincerely,

Gerald R. Ford, M. C.

GRF:1

GERALD R. FORD
FIFTH DISTRICT, MICHIGAN

MICHIGAN OFFICE:
425 CHERRY STREET SE.
GRAND RAPIDS

Congress of the United States
Office of the Minority Leader
House of Representatives
Washington, D.C.

October 18, 1966

Mr. Robert N. Winter-Berger
123 East 75th Street
New York, New York 10021

Dear Bob:

Many thanks for your wonderful contribution to our Kent
County Campaign effort.

I am enclosing a copy of a letter I have sent to Walter
Russell at the Kent County Republican Committee, forwarding
the check and asking him to see that your tickets are ready
to be picked up at 301 McKay Tower in Grand Rapids on
October 25th.

Again, many many thanks and warmest personal regards.

Sincerely,

Gerald R. Ford / M. C.

GRF:l

Enclosure

October 18, 1966

Mr. Walter Russell
Kent County Republican Committee
301 McKay Tower
Grand Rapids, Michigan

Mrs. Timmens
Mrs. Marba Parrett

Dear Walt:

I am enclosing a check from Mr. Robert N. Winter-Berger,
123 East 75th Street, New York, New York 10021, for the
purchase of five tickets for the dinner on October 25th.

Mr. Winter-Berger is planning to be in Grand Rapids for the
dinner and will call for the tickets at your office on
October 25th. Will you please see that the five tickets
are ready for him to pick up on that date.

Warmest personal regards.

Sincerely,

Gerald R. Ford, M. C.

GRF:1

Enclosure

GERALD R. FORD
FIFTH DISTRICT, MICHIGAN

MICHIGAN OFFICE:
425 CHERRY STREET SE.
GRAND RAPIDS

Congress of the United States
Office of the Minority Leader
House of Representatives
Washington, D.C.

Nov. 28, 1966

Mr. Robert Winter Berger
123 E. 75th St.
New York, N.Y., 10021

Dear Bob,

Thank you so much for your recent telegram of congratulations
and best wishes relating to the outcome of the election.

As you know, I couldn't be more pleased with the results, and
your message puts the "frosting" on the cake.

Warmest personal regards.

Sincerely,

Gerald R. Ford, M.C.

GRF:dm

September 25, 1967

Congressman Gerald R. Ford
H. 230
Office of the Minority Leader
The Capitol
Washington, D. C. 20515

Dear Jerry:

As I've mentioned many times in the past, I very much
sympathize with what you are doing in Congress.

To this end, although I realize it is only a drop in the
bucket, I am enclosing a small Money Order drawn to the
order of the Republican Congressional Booster Committee
in the sum of $500.00 -- to help you and the Republican
Party in the forthcoming Congressional Elections in 1968.

In the next few weeks, I expect to make additional contributions of like sums, to show my support for what I
believe to be a noble and necessary cause.

Once again, I remain with many, many thanks for what you
are doing,

                              Yours most sincerely,

                              Robert N. Winter-Berger

RNWB/mn

GERALD R. FORD
FIFTH DISTRICT, MICHIGAN

MICHIGAN OFFICE:
425 CHERRY STREET SE.
GRAND RAPIDS
ZIP 49502

Congress of the United States
Office of the Minority Leader
House of Representatives
Washington, D.C. 20515

September 27, 1967

Mr. Robert N. Winter-Berger
123 East 75th Street
New York, New York 10021

Dear Bob:

Many, many thanks for your most generous contribution to
the Republican Congressional Boosters Club. Your check is
being sent on to the Finance Committee and you should
receive an official acknowledgement very shortly.

I know I speak for all of the Republican Leadership in the
House of Representatives when I express gratitude for your
fine aid and assistance. We are desperately trying to gain
control of the House as you well know so such grand help as
you are giving is deeply appreciated.

Thank you again and warmest personal regards.

Sincerely,

Gerald R. Ford, M. C.

GRF:1

cc: Republican Congressional Boosters

GERALD R. FORD
FIFTH DISTRICT, MICHIGAN

MICHIGAN OFFICE:
425 CHERRY STREET SE.
GRAND RAPIDS
ZIP 49502

Congress of the United States
Office of the Minority Leader
House of Representatives
Washington, D.C. 20515

April 1, 1969

Mrs. Edith Taylor Dunnington
812 Park Avenue
New York, New York 10021

Dear Mrs. Dunnington:

I am deeply grateful for your kind and thoughtful letter of March
28th and your most generous contribution to the Republican Congressional
Committee. Your remarks concerning my Republican leadership in the House
of Representatives are very much appreciated. However, without the aid
and assistance of such good friends and supporters as you and Bob Winter-
Berger as well as others throughout the country, it would not have been
possible to increase our ranks last November.

I am forwarding your check to the Republican Congressional Committee
where you may be sure it will be used to good advantage--either in the
campaign for new members in 1970 or for assisting some of our freshmen
members in taking care of their 1968 campaign debts.

Thank you again for all your wonderful help for our Republican cause and
warmest personal regards.

Sincerely,

Gerald R. Ford, M. C.

GRF:1

THE GERALD FORD LETTERS

Hon. George Romney
Governor of Michigan

KENT COUNTY

REPUBLICAN

FINANCE COMMITTEE

REPUBLICAN
HEADQUARTERS
TELEPHONE
(616) 459-8183

until April 1, 1966
207 HOUSEMAN BUILDING
after April 1, 1966
301 McKAY TOWER
GRAND RAPIDS, MICHIGAN 49502

Hon. Gerald R. Ford
House Minority Leader

EXECUTIVE COMMITTEE
ELLIOTT A. SERAFIN, CHAIRMAN
CARL H. MORGENSTERN, VICE CHAIRMAN
GEORGE MORITZ, TREASURER
GEORGE V. BOUCHER
PETER C. COOK
GEORGE E. COWLISHAW
WENDELL C. DAVIS
LOU M. DEXTER
ROBERT C. C. HEANEY
DONALD J. PORTER
WALTER J. RUSSELL
MRS. HERMAN SCHOONBECK
FLOYD SCHUT
MRS. MARION C. STEKETEE
HERBERT E. TRAPP

COMMITTEE MEMBERS
WESLEY AVES
RALPH B. BALDWIN
JOHN O. BARKWELL
WILLIAM H.BETHUNE DO
THOMAS C. BLOODGOOD JR.
GORDON B. BONFIELD
STEPHEN C. BRANSDORFER
STANLEY J. BYINGTON
NORMAN B. DEGRAAF
BETHUNE DUFFIELD
THEODORE E. DUNN
KENNETH ELLIS
FRANK B. FEHSENFELD
THOMAS G. FORD SR.
R. DALE FRANK
JULIUS FRANKS DDS
RICHARD M. GILLETT
PAUL G. GOEBEL SR.
PAUL G. GOEBEL JR.
WALTER S. GOODSPEED
BRITTON L. GORDON
H. SAMUEL GREENAWALT
ALBERT L. HAMMER
HUGO B. HAMMERSLAG
ROBERT T. HARRISON DO
BRIAN R. HEANEY
ALBERTUS J. HOFFS MD
ROBERT L. HOOKER
ROBERT B. HOWLETT
ALLEN I. HUNTING
IVAR F. JOHNSON
ADOLPH K. KRAUSE
C. LINCOLN LINDERHOLM
J. LESLIE LIVINGSTON
JOHN B. MARTIN
WILLIAM H. MARTINDILL
GERALDINE MASTERS
J. D. MILLER MD
J. PRESTON MILLER
CHARLES E. MILLS
FRANK R. NEUMAN
WILLIAM W. PETERSON
GEORGE RICHEL
FRANCIS T. RUSSELL
ELMER G. SCHAEFER
L. WILLIAM SEIDMAN
ADRIAN VANDENBOUT
JOHN A. VANDONGEN
PHILIP J. VICARI
FREDERICK J. VOGT
MRS. LOUIS WALTZ
MRS. RUTH E. WEBBER
PETER M. WEGE
GEORGE L. YOUNG (GRMUTL)

December 1, 1966

Mr. Robert Winter-Berger
123 E. 75th Street
New York, New York 10021

Dear Mr. Winter-Berger:

Now that the election campaign and major fund-raising drives are over, I have a little more time to send you a very special THANK YOU for your outstanding support of the Republican Party in Kent County.

You have become a member of a small and distinguished group of Kent County Republican "Pacesetters" who donate $500 or more to the Republican cause.

Your good friend Jerry Ford was, of course, re-elected---but this time with a smashing 68.5% of the vote.

Your kind of Party support was a major factor in making this a tremendous Republican year.

Sincerely,

Elliott A. Serafin
Finance Chairman

213

HOUSE OF REPRESENTATIVES
WASHINGTON, D. C.

October 2, 1967

Mr. Robert N. Winter-Berger
123 East 75th Street
New York, N. Y.   10021

Dear Bob,

Thank you so much for your kind and
thoughtful note after Mother's death.   It
was so good of you to write.

Betty and my brothers and their
families join me in expressing appreciation
for your kindness.

Thank you again and warmest personal
regards.

Sincerely,

Gerald R. Ford, M.C.

GERALD R. FORD
FIFTH DISTRICT, MICHIGAN

MICHIGAN OFFICE:
425 CHERRY STREET SE.
GRAND RAPIDS
ZIP 49502

Congress of the United States
Office of the Minority Leader
House of Representatives
Washington, D.C. 20515

February 2, 1968

Mr. Robert N. Winter-Berger
123 East 75th Street
New York, New York 10021

Dear Bob,

I was so pleased to know that David Trapp enjoyed thoroughly
his opportunity to see and hear in person the State of the Union
speech.

Your kind comments about Betty's influence was, of course, deeply
appreciated.

The arrangements for the national convention are being made by
the National Committee. I can only suggest, therefore, that anyone who is interested in obtaining tickets get in touch with the
National Committeeman or National Committeewoman from his state.

As you may know, the National Committeeman for New York is:

> Mr. George L. Hinman
> Room 5600
> 13 Rockefeller Plaza
> New York, New York 10020

The National Committeewoman for New York is:

> Mrs. Keith McHugh
> 10 Gracie Square
> New York, New York 10028

Warmest personal regards.

Sincerely,

Gerald R. Ford, M.C.

GRF:mh

P.S. If I get any tickets I will
keep Dave & you in mind. J.

GERALD R. FORD
FIFTH DISTRICT, MICHIGAN

MICHIGAN OFFICE:
425 CHERRY STREET SE.
GRAND RAPIDS
ZIP 49502

Congress of the United States
Office of the Minority Leader
House of Representatives
Washington, D.C. 20515

August 22, 1968

Mr. Robert N. Winter-Berger
Public Relations Counsel
123 East 75th Street
New York, New York 10021

Dear Bob:

Many, many thanks for your kind and thoughtful letter of
August 14th. Needless to say, I am deeply grateful for
your most gracious comments concerning my chairmanship of
the National Convention. There is naturally a great deal
of tension involved in such an assignment so it is really
good to hear from friends such as you that it came over well.

All in all, I was very pleased with the results. I believe
we have a great ticket and feel very confident that we will
have a fine GOP victory in November.

Thank you also for your wonderful offer of help. My office
has told me of your telephone call prior to the convention
offering your aid and assistance. You are most kind and
you may be sure I am keeping it in mind.

Thank you again for your thoughtfulness in writing and
warmest personal regards.

Sincerely,

Gerald R. Ford, M. C.

GRF:1

GERALD R. FORD
FIFTH DISTRICT, MICHIGAN

MICHIGAN OFFICE:
425 CHERRY STREET SE.
GRAND RAPIDS
ZIP 49502

Congress of the United States
Office of the Minority Leader
House of Representatives
Washington, D.C. 20515

April 23, 1968

Mr. Robert N. Winter-Berger
Public Relations Counsel
123 East 75th Street
New York, N. Y. 10021

Dear Bob,

Many thanks for your letter of April 12 and your interest in
Richard Ball. I do want to be just as helpful as I possibly can.

When Richard does submit his formal application to the Medical School
at the University of Michigan I will be pleased to write the letter
of recommendation. I am impressed with his fine extracurricular
record.

Warmest personal regards.

Sincerely,

Gerald R. Ford, M.C.

GRF:mr

I told the story of Jerry Ford and the Alexander Guterma case in *The Washington Pay-Off*. There is little point in repeating it in these pages.

Here are some of the letters from me to Ford regarding this matter.

Gerald Ford had either the good sense or the good fortune not to put anything in writing on this one.

Giving him all the best of it, I'll attribute it to luck rather than good sense. For I was seeing him regularly, often as much as two and three times a week and always on a warm, intimate basis.

(212) MO. 1-2926

Robert N. Winter-Berger
PUBLIC RELATIONS COUNSEL

123 EAST 75TH STREET
NEW YORK, N. Y. 10021

September 29, 1967

Mr. Richard H. Wels
Moss, Wels & Marcus
341 Madison Avenue
New York, New York 10017

Dear Mr. Wels:

Receipt is hereby acknowledged for the two checks dated
September 20th, 1967, in the sum total of $2,500.00, which
you gave me on September 20th, 1967, in return for which I
have agreed to look into the problem of the remission of
a fine levied on your client, Alexander Guterma, in conjunc-
tion with a prison sentence imposed upon him on February 17th,
1960.

I will do my best to expedite the solution of the aforementioned problem. However, I do not claim to guarantee
anything, and/or to fix anything.

You have asked me to use my best efforts, and have offered
to pay me.

If the foregoing meets with your complete understanding and
approval, would you please sign the enclosed copy and return
it to me.

Sincerely,

Robert N. Winter-Berger

AGREED AND ACCEPTED:

Richard H. Wels

The Gerald Ford Letters

October 6, 1967

Congressman Gerald R. Ford
H. 230
Office of the Minority Leader
The Capitol
Washington, D. C. 20515

Dear Jerry:

I am writing you this letter in reference to a request which I received from a New York Attorney, Richard H. Wels. He asked me to write to you about an unfulfilled promise/made by Senator Robert Kennedy in 1961 - to his client, Alexander Guterma,- when Senator Kennedy was the Attorney General of the United States.

Mr. Wels asked me to write to you specifically, as the Republican Leader of the House of Representatives, rather than as an individual Congressman divorced from your position in the leadership, because this is a matter concerning the reappraisal of some of the promises the current Administration has made in apparent bad faith.

The facts, as presented to me, are rather bizarre, and, if true, in my opinion, would warrant an investigation and/or review of the situation.

On February 17th, 1960, Alexander Guterma was convicted of failing to file a report with the Securities Exchange Commission and the New York Stock Exchange, as a beneficial owner, showing substantial changes in his ownership in the F.L. Jacobs Co. (a Michigan Corp.) - under the Securities Exchange Act of 1934, and of conspiracy to violate this Act. Judge Lloyd MacMahon of the Southern District sentenced him to four years and eleven months, and fined him $160,000 on a total of fifteen counts. Subsequently, two counts were dismissed, and the fine was reduced to $140,000.

In addition to this indictment, which resulted in the above mentioned conviction, Mr. Guterma also had several other indictments pending against him at the time of his sentence.

In due course, Mr. Guterma was duly remanded to the Federal Penitentiary in Atlanta, Georgia. During the fall of 1960, the Assistant U.S. Attorney, Jerome J. Londin, had him transferred back to the Federal House of Detention in New York. It was here, in February of 1961, that Mr. Guterma received a visit from Mr. Walter Sheridan, who was then the Special and Confidential Assistant to Attorney General Kennedy.

220

THE GERALD FORD LETTERS

Congressman Gerald R. Ford   2.

Because of Mr. Guterma's background, and his partnership in business
deals with some of "the Desert Inn crowd", the Department of Justice
felt that Mr. Guterma knew a great deal about this crowd's operations
throughout the United States. Mr. Sheridan wanted his cooperation.
In return for this cooperation, Mr. Sheridan noted that Attorney'
General Kennedy would be willing

> 1. to recommend dismissal of the other pending
>   indictments against Mr. Guterma,
>
> 2. to recommend Mr. Guterma for parole at the
>   earliest possible time,
>
> 3. and to remit his fine of $140,000.

Mr. Wels, as Mr. Guterma's attorney, asked Mr. Sheridan for some
sort of assurance that these three promises would be kept, if his
client cooperated in an unqualified way with the Department of Justice.
Mr. Sheridan agreed; and, in the latter part of May of 1961 in the
Southern District Office of the U.S. Attorney, Mr. Wels received
that assurance directly from Attorney General Kennedy on the telephone.

Mr. Guterma proceeded to tell the Department of Justice everything
he knew. In addition to Mr. Sheridan, he worked with Special
Assistant Attorney General Charles Shaffer, Jr. (now a Washington
attorney), William Hundley, Chief of the Organized Crime Division
at the Department of Justice (now Legal Counsel to the National
Football League), and John Keaney, at present, still in the Criminal
Division of the Department of Justice.

It has been freely admitted in the Department of Justice, that Mr.
Guterma's cooperation and subsequent court room testimony resulted
in most of the major indictments and convictions during Senator
Kennedy's tenure as Attorney General. To mention only a few cases,
Mr. Guterma worked with the Department of Justice on the United Dye
case; his testimony was responsible for the removal, in 1962, of
Ted McCormack as President of the American Stock Exchange (which
grew into the Re and Re case); he was the Government's chief witness
in the Las Vegas "skimoff" investigation of the Nevada crowd in 1962;
he was also the Government's chief witness in the Lionel Corporation
investigation; his testimony resulted in the indictment and conviction of Moe Dalitz for income tax evasion; he testified that a certain
Dr. Robert Erdman was the "bag man" for the Desert Inn crowd in the
New York area; his testimony in the Erdman case resulted in the conviction of Judge Keogh in addition to Dr. Erdman; his testimony was
also responsible for the recall, in 1962, of the then Panamanian
Ambassador to the United States, Eusebio A. Morales, who was taking
mob money out of this country in his diplomatic pouch,- and depositing
it to their account in a Panamanian bank.

Congressman Gerald R. Ford   3.

Special Assistant Attorney General Charles Shaffer, in 1962, met
with Nevada's Governor Sawyer,- to bring to his attention what
the investigations of the Department of Justice had uncovered, in
reference to Las Vegas. They requested, and received, his cooperation.

As I previously noted, there were other indictments pending against
Mr. Guterma, while he was incarcerated. You will recall, the original
promise made by the Attorney General was that these indictments
would be vacated. But, the Department of Justice insisted, finally,
that he would have to plead to a series of counts. They assured him
it would have the same effect, as if the indictments had been dismissed.
This, of course, is not true. Nevertheless, he pleaded guilty to
a series of counts before Judge Herlands in the Southern District,
and, in April of 1963, the Judge sentenced him - but placed him on
probation for five years.

At this trial, Assistant U.S. Attorney Gerald Walpin made a forceful
recommendation to Judge Herlands for clemency, citing Mr. Guterma's
cooperation in the United Dye case. He was the Government's main
witness, and was on the stand for three months. During the course
of the United Dye trial, Judge Herlands, who was also the judge in
this case, noted that he found Alexander Guterma to "be a man of
truth, after having an unusually long time to examine him".

Yet, Attorney General Kennedy had not fulfilled the first of his
three promises.

In April of 1963, Mr. Guterma petitioned the Parole Board for an
early parole. He was turned down. The same day that his parole
was turned down by the Board, Attorney General Kennedy himself asked
for a special meeting later that day. At that second meeting, his
representative, Willian Hundley, explained to the Parole Board that
an early parole, and the remission of the fine was part of an agreement that Attorney General Kennedy had made with Mr. Guterma, in
return for his cooperative testimony. The Board immediately recon-
sidered, and granted the parole.

So, Attorney General Kennedy fulfilled the second of his three
promises.

The third promise, the remission of the fine of $140,000, remains,
to this day, unfulfilled.

Shortly after the Parole Board's final pronouncement in April of 1963,
Mr. Guterma was released from prison. He immediately petitioned
the Attorney General for remission of the fine. Mr. Keaney and Mr.
Hundley, in the process of asking for the fine's remission asked him
to take a pauper's oath; which he did. This request, however, was
turned down then, and ever since by the Chief Assistant U.S. Attorney
for the Southern District, Sylvio Marlow, in apparent disregard of
the commitment that Attorney General Kennedy made to Mr. Guterma.

222

ongressman Gerald R. Ford   4.

n subsequent years, John Keaney has repeatedly petitioned the
.S. Attorney to remit Mr. Guterma's fine, without any success.
e has felt that it was a promise that the Department of Justice
ade, and it should be kept. The question here is, why won't the
dministration honor its promises? Or, why should promises be
ade to a citizen by a member of the Cabinet, if they cannot be
ept in good faith?

enator Robert Kennedy has never denied that he made these pro-
ises. Therefore, it would seem odd that the Administration would
ake the credit for criminal convictions and prosecutions, without
onoring the obligations it made to the individual who was respon-
ible for its highly touted success.

y this time, Mr. Guterma's parole has expired. But by reason of
he open fine, the parole has not be vacated. Although he has
aid his debt to society, the Department of Justice still con-
inues to harrass him. For example, as recently as August of 1967,
hen Mr. Guterma wanted to bring his family to New Jersey, from
heir home in Miami for a wedding, the Department of Justice denied
im permission to travel for any purpose other than official govern-
ent business. Thereupon, Assistant U.S. Attorney, Allan Blumberg,
nowing the facts of the case, called Mr. Guterma to New York to
iscuss the possible installment payment of the fine. Therefore,
e was able to attend the wedding in New Jersey with his family.

he present Administration, or some faction in it, seems intend,
s I've noted, upon harrassing Mr. Guterma, despite the obligations
hey have towards him.

ithin the past month, in order to ascertain his true assets in
eference to the installment payment of the fine, the Department
f Justice has asked the F.B.I. to perform an audit on the books
f the corporation of which Mr. Guterma is an employee. Incidentally,
e has no assets, but his wife is a minor stockholder in this firm.
s you know, a group of F.B.I. auditors is hardly the discrete way
o perform an audit. The very fact that they would swarm over a
orporation,for whom he is working, would ruin him locally. Gossip
preads quickly, and most often erroneously, in a small town. I
ould think that there are many other ways to authenticate the
ccuracy and honesty of an audit other than having the F.B.I. move
n so brazenly and overtly. The company is the I. T. Venus Con-
truction Corp. of Boca Raton, Florida.

he question that Mr. Wels would like to have finally answered is,-
hy the harrassment, and why hasn't the fine been remitted. In other
ords, why haven't the obligations of the Administration been honored?

herefore, I would deeply appreciate it, if you could possibly have
omeone look into this case. Perhaps we might be able to find out

Congressman Gerald R. Ford   5.

just exactly what the Administration has on its mind?

At any rate, anything at all you might uncover in regard to this
mystery would be very deeply appreciated.

                                    Yours most sincerely,

                                    Robert N. Winter-Berger

RNWB/mn

October 31, 1967

Congressman Gerald R. Ford
H. 230
Office of the Minority Leader
The Capitol
Washington, D. C. 20515

Dear Jerry:

I just wanted to write you this short note, for the record.

As I mentioned to Frank Meyer, today, in reference to Alexander
Guterma, he still, at this late date, is acting in the capacity
of a cooperative Government witness. He hopes, that by doing
this, he will continue to live up to his end of the bargain,
according to the agreement that was made on his behalf by his
attorney, Richard Wels, with the then Attorney General, Robert
Kennedy.

For the past two days, he, once again, has been conferring in
New York with Robert Morgenthau, U.S. Attorney for the Southern
District. He has been helping Mr. Morgenthau with one of the
Government prosecutions, by giving the Government much needed
information.

Mr. Morgenthau, incidentally, who knows all of the facts and
injustices of Mr.Guterma's case, it was related to me, told
Mr.Wels, yesterday, that he will cooperate in any way to get
Mr. Guterma his long overdue justice.

Jerry, I would really very deeply appreciate it, under the circumstances, if you could send me some word, at your earliest
convenience. I'd like to be able to advise Guterma what to do.

Hoping this communication finds you in the very best of health
and happiness, I remain, with many, many thanks

Yours most appreciatively,

Robert N. Winter-Berger

RNWB/mn

December 4, 1967

Congressman Gerald R. Ford
Office of the Minority Leader
House of Representatives
Washington, D. C. 20515

Dear Jerry:

I am just writing you this very short note, to gell you how very grateful I am for the advice you gave me the other day.

It was very nice of you - to take the time and effort, and I am more appreciative than I can adequately say.

Your indulgence was extraordinary, and I shall not soon forget it.

However, I hope that you will not forget - that I am ready, willing, and able to work at any time, anywhere, for you and/or the Republican Congressional Committee in regard to the forthcoming National Election.

Once again, with many, many thanks, I remain

Most gratefully yours,

Robert N. Winter-Berger

RNWB/mn

III .

Ford said he met me only a *few* times. I say I met with him hundreds of times. And always on a warm, intimate basis.

We were friends.

Why then, expose him as I have in this book? I would like to quote from *All The President's Men* by Carl Bernstein and Bob Woodward of the *Washington Post*. They describe, in their book, an encounter between attorney Edward Bennett Williams, the *Post*'s lawyer, and Patrick J. Buchanan, the White House speechwriter.

Buchanan was defending Watergate with Williams talking about how dirty it was.

"How about your clients, Ed?" He was referring to James Hoffa, Bobby Baker, Frank Costello, and others.

"How about some of the crooks you defended?" Buchanan taunted.

"There's a big difference," Williams boomed, "such a big difference." He bent his head, leaned against the bar and looked up quietly.

"What's the difference, Ed?"

"I didn't run any of my clients for President."

227

IV

There are many primitive tribes who operate in this fashion: members of the tribe quarrel among themselves. They do every kind of "nastiness" to each other.

Tribesmen take sides. They assist one or the other parties. They try to punish the tribal foe.

But woe be it to any outsider who threatens any member of the tribe. Immediately, the tribe bands together to assault the common enemy.

I became that enemy. I dared to say that I gave ("loaned") Jerry Ford some $15,000 in cash (which I did) and that he worked on my behalf for various of the accounts I secured as a lobbyist (which he did).

He said he wrote to me "no more than five or six times," but you've had a chance to look at more than thrice that many Ford to Winter-Berger letters.

He said that he "may have met me eight or ten times" and here there can be no mistake, no misunderstanding. Jerry is a bold and knowing liar.

V

During and after my appearances before the Senate and House committees, I received widespread publicity in the daily newspapers, weekly magazines, and on television and radio. Most of it was bad.

Most of it said that I had been thoroughly discredited. Some of it suggested that I was deliberately lying.

I was no longer described as a former lobbyist but as a former "influence peddler."

Much was made of the fact that the Senate committee asked the Justice Department to review my testimony before it as well as the Les Whitten affidavit.

Gerald Ford denied everything. Therefore logic would make me a perjurer.

In mid-February, 1974, the assistant attorney-general of the United States, Henry E. Peterson, wrote to Senator Cannon, the committee chairman.

The letter came from Peterson because he was in charge of the criminal division. What a wonderful finale if "the boys on the hill" could indict and imprison me for daring to attack and expose one of their favorite sons!

They were not to enjoy that satisfaction.

Peterson wrote in part, "We have completed our analysis of Mr. Winter-Berger's testimony for possible violations of the law, including perjury. After considering all the evidence and attendant circumstances, we have concluded that the facts of this case are not such as to warrant prosecutive action . . ."

The news about the letter was buried in the tenth paragraph of a general story that was published in the *Newark Sunday Star-Ledger*. It appeared on page nine.

To my knowledge—and I have carefully combed the news weeklies and half a hundred daily newspapers—not another word about this story appeared anywhere else.

It was headlines when I was accused of perjury.

But it didn't rate even one line on the obituary page when I was "cleared" by the U.S. attorney-general's office.

VI

It is my earnest belief that the United States of America is suffering both presently and for its future. Suffering because we are in the hands of a kakistocracy: a government or rule by the worst.

With the rare exception of a Judge Sirica, we have no heroes. The givers and the takers have driven decent people out of government.

Recent events have shown that senators and congressmen and even the president and vice-president of the United States can be bought and sold.

When I said this in *The Washington Pay-Off*, I was not taken seriously. We don't like mud thrown at our tin gods.

Six months after I met Jerry Ford, he remarked, "Money is the name of the game. Without it, you're dead."

Robert N. Winter-Berger

New York City
May 10, 1974

230

INDEX